NEWNES ALL COLOUR GUIDE

Golf

BERNARD COOKE

NEWNES BOOKS

Dedication

To David, Elizabeth, Richard and Alison.
To Audrey without whom it would never have been written and to
Peter my late son who couldn't stay until it was.

The Foreword

The year 1968 holds a special memory for me. It was the year I
organized a group of American Junior golfers to tour the famous golf
courses of Scotland and England.
It was also the year I was invited to give a golf clinic in London to
a small but interested group of British professionals. The clinic was
an idea of Percy Huggins of *Golf Monthly*. One of the professionals
was Bernard Cooke.
I was immediately impressed by the fire with which this man
pursued golf knowledge. It almost matched his red hair! So much
golf information is personal opinion – Bernard Cooke would accept
only scientific facts.
In the years that have followed I have read everything Bernard has
put on paper and my knowledge has been enriched. His exposure,
through magazine articles, has established him as an authority on
golf instruction. He was honoured in December 1972 when he was
invited to participate in the first all-teaching golf school held by the
Professional Golfers' Association of America at Riviera Beach,
Florida. Each year he travels to Sweden where he instructs students
in that country, making his reputation international.
It is my pleasure to advise any golfer interested in improving his
game to read this authoritative, instructional book.
Bernard Cooke will help you to enjoy a better game!

Irvine E. Schloss
member
The Professional Golfers' Association of America
The Professional Golfers' Association of Great Britain
Golf Writers' Association of America.

Acknowledgements

Percy Huggins who set me on the road to writing.
Malcolm Campbell who steered me to colour photography.
The members of Abridge Golf & Country Club who have always given me such
encouragement.
Irv Schloss my friend and mentor.
John Howard, Groom & Pickerill and Damian Grint for their help and advice.

Bengt Thermaenius of Örebro, Sweden,
who provided the feathery ball.

Photography by Bernard Cooke.

Illustrations
Photography by Bernard Cooke
Photographs and artwork © copyright Newnes
Books with the exception of
Front cover: Bernhard Langer (Allsport/
Dave Cannon)
Back cover: Severiano Ballesteros (Phil Sheldon)

Published by Newnes Books
a division of The Hamlyn Publishing Group
Limited
69 London Road, Twickenham
Middlesex, England TW1 3SB
and distributed for them by
Octopus Distribution Services Limited
Rushden, Northamptonshire NN10 9RZ,
England

Text © copyright Bernard Cooke 1984

Fourth impression 1987

ISBN 0 600 35748 1
Printed in Italy

CONTENTS

THE HISTORY OF THE GAME

The common but simple objectives of every player of golf since the game began are to try to hit a ball with one of several different levers of varying lengths and of varying degrees of tilt to their striking surfaces and to propel it in the straightest possible line for the greatest possible distance with the least possible effort. Also, to make the fewest possible strokes and obtain the lowest possible score on the course they are about to play.

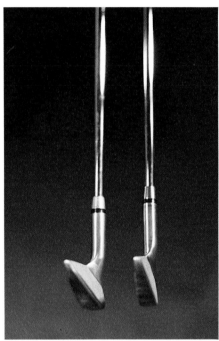

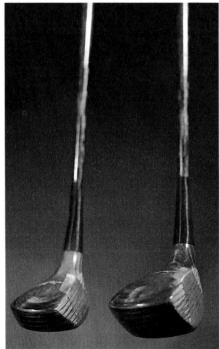

Above: The complete set of irons. Top right: The shortest iron excluding the putter is a sand iron (left) and the longest a 1 iron (right) showing the head sizes and face angles. Right: the longest and shortest woods.

The History of Golf

There is not a great deal that can be said about the history of golf in a few pages. I am, therefore, limiting myself largely to the early history of the game and although what I have to say is neither exhaustive nor original, I hope that readers will find at least some of it interesting. I am much indebted for most, though not quite all, of what I have to say to an ancient volume called *Golf: a Royal and Ancient Game*, edited by Robert Clark and first published in 1875.

According to several sources, including the Roman poet Martial, there was in the days of the Roman Empire a popular game called 'Paganica', derived from the word *paganus* meaning 'a countryman'. This game, it appears, was played with a ball made of leather stuffed with feathers, and a bent stick. It is unfortunate that no adequate description of this game is to be found, and it is perhaps a little fanciful, though not impossible, to suppose that golf in its earliest form was introduced to Britain and elsewhere by the Roman legionaries, many of whom were undoubtedly 'pagani'.

In the thirteenth century in England, reference is made to a game of 'cambuc', which was played with a small wooden ball and a curved stick. This game may have borne some resemblance to golf. Cambuc was one of a number of 'vain games' discouraged by royal authority in order that the time thus wasted should be devoted to improving military skill.

In Scotland, James II in 1457 ordered that 'Football and golf be utterly cried down' and, in the interests of military efficiency, were not to be played again. James III in 1471 and James IV in 1491 repeated such prohibitions. It looks, therefore, as if golf was fairly well established in Scotland by this time. Yet, an earlier act of 1424, discouraging football, golf is not mentioned. Though not of course conclusive, it does suggest that golf had increased substantially in popularity, to say the least, between 1424 and 1457. In any case, golf must have soon acquired an attraction for members of the royal family, for there is a record to the effect that in 1502 James IV paid 14 Scots shillings (roughly about 2 shillings in the English currency of the same period) for clubs from a 'bower' in Perth, and in 1503, got 42 Scots shillings from his Lord High Treasurer to pay a golfing debt.

Across the border, Catherine of Aragon, the unfortunate first of Henry VIII's six wives, mentions golf in a letter of 1513 to Cardinal Wolsey. The relation of the golf mentioned in this letter to the earlier cambuc is not clear. But it is not improbable that this English golf had been imported from Scotland, the ground having been prepared, so to speak, by the older game of cambuc. We can only speculate about this, however.

Crossing the channel, there is evidence that a game called 'Het Kolven' or 'the Golfing' was played in Holland in the early sixteenth century, both on the ground and on the ice – in fact, as conditions permitted. The word 'Kolf', was pronounced 'golf' in spite of being spelt with a 'K', and meant the 'weapon' with which the game was played. Kolf is apparently derived from the Teutonic word 'Kolbe', meaning a club. The ball used was a leather one, stuffed with feathers. The Scottish scholar Andrew Lang's opinion was that the Scots game of golf was not derived from Het Kolven, but both Scotland and England had many contacts with the continent at this period, and it seems very probable that the games in the three countries were connected in some way. However, there can be no doubt that golf was flourishing in Scotland in the seventeenth century. Indeed, it was so popular that it interfered with the proper observance of the Sabbath. In 1592, Edinburgh Town Council forbade any pastimes or games within or without the town upon the Sabbath day, such as golf, etc.

In 1608 John Henrie, Pat Bogie and others were 'accused for playing of the golf on the Links of Leith every Sabbath the time of the sermons, notwithstanding oft admonition past before; were convicted of 20 pounds each one of them, and ordered to be warded [put in prison] until the same were paid, and to find caution not to do the like again at no time hereafter, under the pain of 100 pounds'. James VI of Scotland and I of England was a golfer and established the game at Blackheath in 1608. On his return to Scotland in 1618, James apparently took a lenient view of this profanation of the Sabbath, provided

it was after the ending of all Divine service, and provided Divine service had been attended, though golf is not specifically mentioned in this connection. Charles I was playing golf on Leith Links when he received the news of the Irish rebellion, and again, it is said, at Newcastle in 1640 or 1641, just before Newcastle was occupied by the Scots.

James II appears to have been a regular player. When he was Duke of York he took part in the first international match between 1681 and 1682:

'Two Englishmen, who, during their attendance at the Scottish Court, had, among other fashionable amusements of the period, occasionally practised golf, were one day debating the question with His Highness Duke of York, whether that amusement were peculiar to Scotland or England, and having some difficulty in coming to an issue on the subject, it was proposed to decide the question by an appeal to the game itself, the Englishmen

The 'feathery' ball was in use until nearly 1850. It was a leather-pannelled stitched case stuffed tightly with 2.7 pennyweights of boiled feathers. Patersone would undoubtedly have used one in his historical match. The feathers were superseded in 1848 by the gutty ball, a solid piece of gutta percha rubber, which at the turn of the century was displaced by the elastically wound Haskell ball with a balata cover. Now, the solid ball with an outer cover is back in vogue, but the material is an undisclosed formula.

'Tis an ill wind that blows nobody good. The grey skies and east winds of yesterday were bad for Ascot, but they were appropriate enough over the bleak and sandy undulation of Blackheath where the golfers had come to compete for their summer medal. Many of the hardy Scotchmen who came out in their scarlet jackets and white breeches must have fancied they were home again, that they were playing on the famous links of St Andrews, or by the fair city of Perth, or within sight of Salisbury Crags.'
(From the *Daily News*, June 1874)

agreeing to rest the legitimacy of their national pretensions as golfers, together with a large sum of money, on the result of a match, to be played with his Highness and any Scotchman he could bring forward.

'The Duke, whose great aim at that time was popularity, thinking this is no bad opportunity, both to asserting his claim to the character of a Scotchman, and for flattering a national prejudice, immediately accepted the challenge; and, in the meantime, caused diligent inquiry to be made as to where the most efficient partner was to be found. The person recommended to him for this purpose was a poor man, named John Patersone, a shoemaker, who was not only reputed the best golf player of his day, but whose ancestors had been equally celebrated from time immemorial.

'On the matter being explained to him, Patersone was not quite satisfied as to how he should be able to acquit himself in such great company, but on the Duke encouraging him he said he would do his best.

'The match was played, in which the Duke was, of course, completely victorious, and the shoemaker was dismissed with a reward corresponding to the importance of his service, being an equal share of the stake played for.

'With this money he immediately built himself a comfortable house in the Canongate, upon the wall of which the Duke caused an escutcheon to be affixed, bearing the arms of the family of Patersone.'

The game was played mostly on the 'links' or stretches of grass, sand and gorse along the East coast, although there is evidence that by the beginning of the seventeenth century, if not before, golf was played at Perth and Stirling. The courses, if indeed one can use the word, must have been very rough indeed, and there was no proper body of rules before 1744. St Andrews, lying between pasture on one side and whins, or gorse, on the other, was probably typical. Here, players coming out and coming in played to the same holes, those coming in having priority over those coming out at the same time. Later, when more people were playing, the fairways were widened and holes for going in cut opposite those going out, and this is the origin of the great double greens that are such a characteristic feature of St Andrews Old Course.

It may interest those who know the Old Course in its present form to know that it used to be played by going out on the left and coming home on the right, looking from the town – that is, as a slicer's course rather than a hooker's course. At one time, the course was played left handed one week and right handed the next, to

reduce wear, and at the present time, the course is often turned inside out during part of the winter, for the same reason. But this is rather a digression, and we must return to the eighteenth century.

In 1744 the Company of Gentlemen Golfers (which after 1800 became The Honourable Company of Edinburgh Golfers) was founded, playing on Leith Links, and provided the first code of rules. After considerably more than a century at Leith, the Company was wound up. Fortunately it was revived in 1837, playing at Mussleburgh until 1891. It then acquired the ground near Gullane which, as Muirfield, became and still is, one of the finest golf courses and one of the best tests of golf in the world.

The novelist Tobias Smollett had evidently been impressed by the playing of the game at Leith, for in *The Expedition of Humphry Clinker*, 1771, he gives us the following delightful account:

'I never saw such a concourse of genteel company at any races in England, as appeared on the course at Leith. Hard by, in the fields called The Links, the citizens of Edinburgh divert themselves at a game called golf, in which they use a curious kind of bats tipt with horn, and small elastic balls of leather, stuffed with feathers, rather less than tennis balls, but of a much harder consistence. This they strike with such force and dexterity from one hole to another, that they will fly to an incredible distance. On this diversion the Scotch are so fond that, when the weather will permit, you may see a multitude of all ranks, from the Senator of Justice to the lowest tradesman, mingled together in their shirts, and following the balls with the utmost eagerness. Among others, I was shown one particular set of golfers, the youngest of whom was turned of fourscore. They were all gentlemen of independent fortunes, who had amused themselves with this pastime for the best part of a Century without ever having felt the least alarm from sickness or disgust; and they never went to bed without having each the best part of a gallon of claret in his belly. Such uninterrupted exercise, co-operating with the keen air from the sea, must, without doubt, keep the appetite always on edge, and steel the constitution against all common attacks of distemper.'

One would like to feel that these robust characters belonged to the forerunners of the Honourable Company of Edinburgh Golfers, for they were surely worthy of the designation 'Honourable Company'.

In 1754, the Society of St Andrews Golfers (later the Royal and Ancient Golf Club) was founded, undoubtedly following the example of the Company, and provided a code of rules almost identical

The Golfer's Land

with the first code drawn up by the Company of Gentlemen Golfers and certainly borrowed from it. After William IV granted the Society the title of Royal and Ancient and became its patron, the club gradually assumed the position of the undisputed leader and arbiter of the game. It may seem a curious thing to golfers that the famous Dr Johnson reports a visit to St Andrews in his 'journey to the Western Isles of Scotland', 1773, and yet says nothing about golf. One might have expected at least a censorious comment.

The nineteenth century, especially the second half, saw a rapid extension of the game, and many of the most famous clubs were founded during this period. I will mention only two: Prestwick, founded in 1851, which, with support from the R and A Club, was responsible for starting the Open Championship in 1860. The trophy was the belt that young Tom Morris won three times in succession from 1868 to 1870, and made his own. And the Royal Liverpool Club founded in 1869, which, in 1885, was responsible for an Open Amateur Tournament, the forerunner of the Amateur Championship.

'In the Canongate of Edinburgh, on the wall of a very ancient looking house is a tablet, bearing the following coat – armorial: Three pelicans Vulned: On a Chief three mullets. Crest – a dexter hand grasping a golf club – Motto, "Far And Sure".'
(From *Golf, a Royal and Ancient Game* Macmillan & Co 1893)

THE HISTORY OF THE RULES

I should like to say something very briefly about the history of the rules of the game. The first code of rules was that of the Company of Gentlemen Golfers in 1774 and consisted of the following:

1. You must tee your ball within a club's length of the hole [teeing grounds were not mentioned until 1875 and not defined as such until 1893].

2. Your tee must be upon the ground.

3. You are not to change the ball you strike off the tee.

4. You are not to remove stones, bones or any break-club for the sake of playing your ball except upon the fair green, and that only within a club's length of your ball.

5. If your ball come among water, or any watery filty, you are at liberty to take out your ball and bring it behind the hazard, and teeing it you may play it with any club and allow your adversary a stroke for so getting out your ball.

6. If your balls be found anywhere touching one another you are to lift the first ball, till you play the last.

7. At holing, you are to play your ball honestly for the hole, and not to play on your adversary's ball, not lying in your way to the hole [aggression against one's opponent's ball was thus specifically forbidden].

8. If you should lose your ball by its being taken up, or any other way, you are to go back to the spot where you struck last and drop another ball and allow your adversary a stroke for the misfortune.

9. No man at holing his ball is to be allowed to mark his way to the hole with his club or anything else.

10. If a ball be stopped by any person, horse, dog or anything else, the ball so stopped must be played where it lies.

11. If you draw your club in order to strike, and proceed so far in the stroke as to bring down your club, if then your club shall break in any way, it is to be accounted a stroke.

12. He whose ball lies farthest from the hole is obliged to play first.

13. Neither trench, ditch or dyke made for the preservation of the links, not the Scholars' holes, or the Soldiers lines, shall be accounted a hazard, but the ball is to be taken out, teed and played with any iron club. [This last rule though recurring in the 1754 St Andrews code, obviously applied particularly to Leith, and its recurrence in the St Andrews code is strong evidence that this code was taken over from the Company.]

There is no reference in these 1744 rules to playing the ball as it lies, except under the exceptional circumstances indicated in rule 10. I think we must assume, however, that this principle was so generally accepted as to require no affirming. There is no rule against improving the lie or stance. This was not dealt with until the Aberdeen code of 1783. For most of the rules, no penalty is prescribed. Further criticism and comment on early rules is to be found in Clapcott's book *Some Comments on the Articles and Laws in Playing Golf*, 1945.

I cannot give an account of the development of the rules, but I shall mention a few interesting points. The 1775 rules of the Honourable Company rephrase the rule about 'touching' balls to cover balls lying within 6in (15.2cm), thus originating the stymie rule. This code also indicated that the ball must be played as it lies. 'Out of bounds' was not provided for until 1899, and it is interesting to find references to the fact that after the railway came to St Andrews and ran along the right side of the sixteenth fairway, before 'out of bounds' was defined, shots were played from the railway line sometimes, with astonishing success. The penalty for going out of bounds was prescribed in 1899 as distance only. In 1920, this became stroke and distance. In 1950, it again became distance only. Now it is once more stroke and distance.

At the present time, the Royal and Ancient Club is the court of decision in matters of rules. This position dates officially from 1897, when the Rules of Golf Committee was established by general agreement. This Committee consists of fifteen members of the R and A Club. Its powers are limited to dealing with proposals relating to, or questions of interpretation arising from, the rules and customs of golf. Any resolution to amend or repeal an existing rule or make a new rule has to be carried by a majority and no resolution can be authoritative unless it is endorsed by a two-thirds majority of Club members present at a general meeting.

Present Rules

There are forty-one rules in the present R & A code, which are subdivided into over 200 clauses.

There are thirty-six definitions which are subdivided into over fifty clauses.

There are three appendices containing over twenty clauses covering local rules, design of clubs and the ball, together with two rules of Amateur Status which have more than forty subdivisions.

There are seven rules of etiquette also with subdivisions. From time to time some of the rules are amended. It may not by any means be a triennial ritual, but the changes brought about over the year are probably spaced into the nature of that sort of time. The copyright of the Rules of Golf, incidentally, is jointly owned by the Royal and Ancient Golf Club of St Andrews, Scotland and the United States Golf Association.

It would be nigh on impossible, to record here the extent of the golf rules and dwell on their multiple facets, as this would be well outside the scope of this book.

Consequently I have no hesitation in shelving responsibility for the rules in general to two excellent publications: A

Charles I, while playing golf on Leith Links in October 1641, receives news of the Irish Rebellion.
(From *Golf, a Royal and Ancient Game* Macmillan & Co 1893)

pocket-size free booklet ideal for your golf bag and published by a well-known Insurance Company, who for years have taken on republication whenever changes have been ordained. For ease of study and illustrated clarity I keep and use a copy of *Golf Rules Illustrated* published by Munro-Barr, available through your Golf pro or direct from *Golf Monthly*.

Nowhere in the rules of golf is it mooted that thou shalt not cheat, but that thou shalt not conspire to cheat either with your partner or your opponent. This shines as a beacon, which illuminates the morals of your play and is the cats-eyes that guide you along the straight and narrow roads of golfing honesty.

Professional players on the whole have not enjoyed an unsullied reputation where the rules are concerned. Only very recently a shocking case occurred of one superstar accusing another superstar of cheating. This happened during a major event which carried fabulous prize money. Although there were denials of the intensity of the outburst, it had unfortunately passed through the TV microphone. In all likelihood the accused had no intention of transgressing the law, but the affair mushroomed into golfing globe proportions and added another postscript to the unpleasant side of golfing history.

There was also the sad case of Roberto Vicenzo playing with Tommy Aaron in the US Masters in 1968. He signed his card for a four at a par three at which he took only three. He forfeited his right to play off for the title, which was ultimately won by Bob Goalby. A golfer is not only responsible for making a score but also ascertaining that it is correctly marked – a hard game indeed.

There are professionals who have been known to disqualify themselves from major tournaments for breaches of rules that only they were aware of. In these cases the local rules committee had no option but to endorse the disqualifications. There is no reward for honesty in a case like that. Breaking rules, unwittingly, it is assumed, does not always mean disqualification. Extra stroke penalties are added to your score and for some contingencies you may have to play again from where the offending stroke was made.

In my opinion the seven rules of etiquette should be learned by heart by every golfer and from time to time he or she should undergo a test, which, if it is failed would mean an L plate ignominiously attached to their golf bag or trolley until they eventually satisfy their examiners.

The code of etiquette, or to put it more strongly – *ethics*, should be as important to golfers as the Highway Code is to motorists.

I cannot detail the rules of etiquette here, but a twelve-point synopsis of this code of courtesy is as follows:

1. Have consideration of your fellow players.
2. Do not dawdle between shots. This will leave you with more time to play your shots with the due consideration required. I once followed Palmer for a whole round at Wentworth. I had to run to keep up with his rapid pace of walking between shots. Yet in my younger days I was known as the 'greyhound of the links' by colleagues.
3. Do not deliberately drive into the player ahead. A golf ball is a lethal weapon. In the United States such needless risk could find you at the receiving end of a lifetime's crippling lawsuit.
4. If you are not keeping up with the course traffic, allow it to overtake as you would on a narrow road. What is more, when you have waved those behind on, let them overtake, don't suddenly step on the accelerator.
5. When you have finished a hole get on to the next tee. The practice putting green in front of the Clubhouse is there for that purpose, do not use the greens on the course.
6. If your opponent has won a hole then he should be given the courtesy of playing first on the next hole.
7. You are non-existent as a lone player. Two players take precedence over three or four but, if a match is losing ground to the extent of a complete hole or more, penalties can be imposed and, in any case, you should allow the players you are obviously impeding to go ahead of you.
8. Keep quiet and keep out of their line of flight when other people are playing, just as you would wish them to do when you are playing.
9. Care of the course is not the least of a player's responsibilities and divots (pieces of turf) that have been torn up by ploughing irons should be put back to knit and grow again in their natural surroundings. Footmarks and clubmarks in sand bunkers must be smoothed over again. These days many clubs are generous enough to supply rakes beside these sand hazards for this purpose, otherwise use your sand-iron. The pros are quite skilful with their feet at clearing their imprints in the sand. There is nothing so annoying as having to play a shot from the hole in the sand made by the heel mark you failed to repair during your last round.
10. Replace the flagstick in the hole with as much care as you would when repairing the indentation your ball made when it pitched on the green.
11. Keep your bag and trolley away from the greens, the bunkers and the tees. Keep those buggies further away still.
12. Finally, use a bit of rough, there's some near every tee, for practising swinging. It is good for your wrists. Observation of etiquette will not only improve your game, it could help to keep down the cost of playing, in either subscriptions or green fees, or at the very least minimize the inevitable increase of cost.

EQUIPMENT

In the 1920s, when hickory shafts were the vogue, most of the golf clubs were made in the workshops of the club professionals. With the advent of steel, the professional clubmaker largely ceased making clubs, although in fact, it was easier to make steel-shafted clubs than wooden ones. Because they did not seem to grasp this, they relinquished a very important authority they held in the game.

Custom clubmaking virtually disappeared, and it was only as late as the 1970s, and as a somewhat desperate answer to the increasing number of 'bucket shops' both in the USA and in the UK, that a few professional experts realized that clubmaking with steel shafts was not an insuperable problem for the small craftsman. New machines solved the previous handmaking problems.

From then on custom clubmaking began to re-emerge. It was headed in the USA by Irvine Schloss, who is not only one of the world's top teachers and a fine player but also, as one Canadian professional put it, 'A genius with machine tools'.

He designed an iron head with a hole in the toe that could be variably weighted to suit any specific player. It simply needed a

shaft fixing to it that would also suit the player concerned, together with a grip of the right thickness or thinness.

He designed a machine that could calibrate the loft (the angle at which the clubhead lies in relation to the shaft) of an iron club to suit the individual, a flexboard to test shaft flex, sanding machines and swingweight machines and a host of electrically driven devices to facilitate clubmaking to a customers' specification.

It was Schloss who inaugurated The Professional Golf Club Repairmen's Association of America and I am very proud to be its United Kingdom's representative. My clubmaker Glyn Rowland spent some time in America learning the trade, and now turns out an average of nearly one hundred sets of customized clubs a year made by him and an assistant, Billy Knowles, who is an artist at refurbishing 'old masters'.

History is probably in the course of repeating itself, 'Small', as Schumacher said, 'is beautiful'. The time has come round again for a greater appreciation of the individual craftsman. It certainly has in the United States. Maybe it won't be

long before the United Kingdom follows suit.

The photos show my own 'cottage industry' at work as well as some beautiful examples of the custom clubmakers' art.

Custom-made clubs need not be too expensive. In fact, they can be generally well below the wholesale price of the imported mass-produced sets. This is really excellent value for clubs that are carefully made to measure in every detail.

No assembly line organization could afford to go into the intricacies of, for example, weighting clubs especially to suit the demands of the graphite shaft; yet, given the flex, head weight, dead weight and swing weight, the right graphite shaft for you could add yards to your shots!

That is not to say that the right steel shaft could not also 'multiply the metres' in a club that has had the loving care of a skilled and experienced craftsman.

For the beginner the choice of clubs must present quite a difficulty. Beware the attractions of the cut-price stores. They can leave you with a mass of scrap metal of no golfing use to you whatsoever. Make for your nearest Golf Club and visit the golf professional's shop there. The ul-

Opposite: The wood neck is drilled not only to fit the shaft but at an angle that will determine the lie of the club.

Below: After the swing weight and disc have been glued into the toe hole on the iron head, the club is clamped on to our specially made rack for drying.

The Schloss-designed iron head, showing the toe hole for the swing weight. Most of the assembly line clubs have the swing weights glued into the bottom of the shaft at the neck of the club with their many attendant disadvantages.

timate is the made to measure set. You would never regret having a set made to fit you.

It is not necessary to buy a complete set as soon as you decide you are going to play golf.

Your first requirement would be a 6-iron followed by an 8-iron and then a wedge. You should then graduate to a 4-wood, then a 2-wood and after this a 4-iron.

Within a matter of months or weeks if you show some latent talent, you will want to add the 'odd numbers'.

A custom clubmaker can make all these for you so that whichever you choose last, odds or the evens, they will still perfectly match the ones you bought formerly.

You'll need a putter. Go into the pro's shop. He won't be worth his salt if he doesn't let you try any of his selection on the Club's practice putting green. The one you like will be the one you will putt with.

You're going to need golf balls, of course – and more than one or two, in fact, between twenty and thirty. There are two sizes, British, which is 1.62 in (4.11 cm) and the slightly larger American, which is 1.68 in (4.26 cm). Just as the change from wooden to steel golf shafts provided a historical milestone, so did the

changes from the feathery to the solid to the 'wound' golf ball provide a similar landmark. Strangely enough, there has now been a reversion to the solid ball, which is considered to be far more controllable.

You will need a pair of spiked shoes, either metal spiked or rubber spiked, as a very important part of your equipment. So many people demur from buying good golf shoes. It is worthwhile remembering that you will be shod with these for up to four or more hours of playing, which involves a lot of walking and tacking uphill and down dale. Also your feet will be affected by the whims and vagaries of weather: rain, snow or a blistering June sun. Your feet support your golf swing as well as you, so provide generously for their comfort.

You are obviously not going to swing well in an overcoat. There are plenty of trousers, sweaters and shirts especially designed for golfers. These must protect and allow freedom of movement. An umbrella is a must but don't, whatever you do, play golf in an electric storm. Remember you are carrying a set of lethal conductors. You may never get to the last hole, on the other hand you may! Even the rules of golf allow you shelter from lightning.

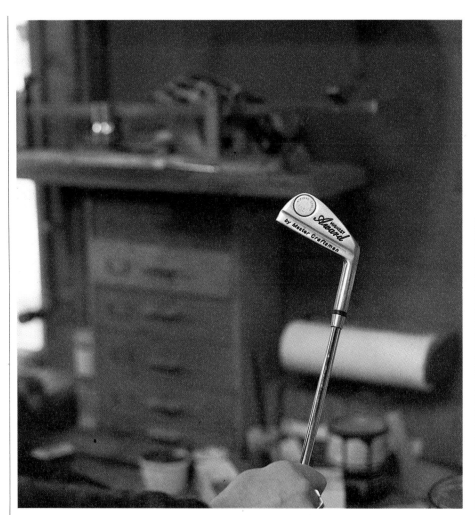

Left: A finished iron.

Below: A finished wood.

Bottom: The complete set.

NICKLAUS TEACHES WATSON

Surely the superstars don't need golf lessons? Who could possibly teach them? There are very few, if any, of the top golfers, even such legends as Jack Nicklaus and Tom Watson, who do not have their own particular coach.

Whilst they are on tour they tend to correct each other, or pop into the teaching professional located nearest to the tournament venue.

Sevvy Ballesteros is ever under the watchful eyes of his brother Manuel. I have seen Bernard Langer of West Germany lending a ready ear to Torston Giedeon his colleague and compatriot, and Giedeon being corrected in his swing by Langer.

The Japanese group practised together and you needn't be fluent in Japanese to surmise that there is a lot of mutual assistance going on as they fire shot after shot down the practice fairway.

When I am taking photographs on the practice grounds at the tournaments I visit for the particular purpose of illustrating my writing, it is not unusual for a player to beckon me over and seek my advice on his swing.

Hugh Baiocchi of South Africa, Baldovino Dassu of Italy are two of my 'regulars' among others who like to have a 'key' to keep them swinging well for the ensuing event.

Keys or props play an important part in giving a player something to concentrate on, at the same time improving the function of their swing mechanics. Sometimes the keys are only gimmicks. A player can be swinging well and not *feel* that he is. A good teacher can introduce a gimmick, or placebo, which convinces the player that this is the very thing to put him right. It works because he believes it will.

Real faults can be analyzed quite effectively from the feedback of the type of golf ball flight a swing is producing. The corrections restore the players skill and his

'Set yourself up', Nicklaus demands. 'Let me check your aim and your grip.'

confidence soars. One of the arts of teaching is using one correction to put right more than one fault.

Perhaps the most exclusive lesson it was ever my privilege to observe took place at Walton Heath during the Ryder Cup in 1981. It was Jack Nicklaus, the world's number one player, teaching Tom Watson, potentially the world's next number one player.

Watson was certainly off form at Walton Heath during that International match. Nicklaus must have spent nearly three hours going through the rudiments of the golf swing.

Tom Watson expressed to Nicklaus his concern that he should think only of the movement and disregard what happened to the ball. 'I'm just not going to care about the shot', said Nicklaus. 'Only how I intend to concentrate on my swing.'

Nicklaus demonstrated all the swing parts – then the whole. He grabbed Watson's head. Checked his backswing. Made him hold his finish. He took him back through the ABC of his golf swing.

No one should be ashamed of starting with the alphabet and what is more, constantly referring back to it. If Tom Watson can, there is positively no reason why anyone else shouldn't.

I am never very happy about the hordes of amateur teachers who emanate from the thousands of world-wide Golf

Top: Nothing escapes Nicklaus's eagle eye as grip and stance assembly are closely scrutinized.

Left: Now to the top of your backswing and we will check your coil and lateral and vertical extension.

Above: 'A little more wrist cock, like this, Tom,' Nicklaus demonstrates – 'Outside the line'.

Top left: 'I feel I am coming over the top, I can't control my downswing path, Jack.'
Top right: And then I go inside through the ball.
Above: 'Take your hands back like this, Tom, not quite so upright.
Right: Watch this swing.

Clubs. I realise, of course, that ninety-nine percent of these are motivated purely by human kindness. They are only trying to help. Alas, in too many cases they are about as helpful as Stan Laurel was to Oliver Hardy in their comic film stories.

In 1972 I spent some time with USA coach Irv Schloss. I shall never forget one particular morning when I was watching him teach. Not more than 20 yd (9 m) away from his pitch were two rather elderly people, obviously husband and wife. For half an hour or so the husband was 'teaching' the wife. Whenever the ball was contacted, which was rarely, it merely rolled a few yards along the ground at a tangent from where she was aiming. Then they reversed roles. She began teaching him. The results were not quite so good. He missed more than he hit and he was a little short on length compared to his wife.

All this 20 yd away from one of, if not *the* leading teacher in America and even beyond.

We all need teaching and we all especially need good teachers, together with any good advice that will help us progress in this fascinating and challenging game.

This page: And as my roving camera reports, this 'pro teaching pro' phenomenon extends into the European tour camp as well.

WATSON QUALITIES

There are so many qualities needed to be a superstar that it is surprising anyone could have the luck to be born with them. It certainly must need superhuman abilities to acquire them.

You are not going to need all the fifteen virtues set out below, some physical some psychological, to play golf, but a knowledge of these will allow you to reflect on your achievable goals and perhaps save the inevitable disappointment of failing to reach to the stars when in fact the relative enjoyment of the down-to-earth monthly medals are well within your grasp. Here are a selection of the outstanding qualities (there are more), which players like Watson and others possess.

1. A strong physique is a decided advantage, but it is not always the biggest player who wins.

2. It is important to be able to aim properly.

3. Continuity of pace combined with accurate sequence of movement.

4. The ability to move swiftly without effort.

5. The compacted muscular power that can be exerted within the shown time lapse of less than two seconds, the time a golf swing takes at the top level.

6. The muscular energy that can be used in one particular swing segment of the whole movement.

7. Eye, hand, clubhead and ball co-ordination.

8. Agility – for example the strength required to accurately change swing direction.

9. Balance.

10. A kinesthetic sensitivity that can be interpreted as 'knowing what is going on'. If you have to twist your arms – you *know* you are twisting your arms.

11. A repetitive rhythm – effortless and unhurried.

12. Dexterity – control of hands in particular. Not separately, but acting in unison.

13. Physical stamina and fitness, including mental alertness.
14. Adaptability – performing with equal skill under varying conditions.
15. The ability to practise.

If you look at my photographs of the Watson swing sequence, his movements appear to be remarkably simple. It is worth noting that these fourteen pictures are a selection of over eighty taken from the same shot. It will give you an idea of the speed at which he was moving when I tell you that my camera was running at sixty-four frames per second. He took less than two seconds to play the shot. You could certainly add *speed* to those fifteen qualities of Watson's.

You can try to emulate the Watson movement. In fact, in the coming pages we will take the common factors of the superstars and superimpose them on you.

I would not want you to run away with the idea that you will end up playing golf like Tom Watson, Arnold Palmer, Tony Jacklin or any of the other superstars. Imitation does not necessarily completely close the gap between skills but it can narrow it down a lot. At this point I should remind you that it is very easy to confuse style with method. I remember someone coming to me for coaching who was a Lee Trevino fanatic. As I walked down to the practice ground, I saw that from a distance he certainly looked like Lee Trevino. Not only did he wear Trevino-like clothes, but he was about the same physique. He believed he had adopted the same swing technique but he wasn't getting very good results.

The fact was, he had adopted Trevino's *style*: his characteristics or idiosyncracies, but not Trevino's *method*. There is quite a difference. Looking like a certain player will not contribute one iota to closing the skill gap. Adopting his method will.

Watson's method like the other 'greats' past and present, contains certain common factors:

At address or assembly, his posture is upright. His left arm and club shaft are in good alignment. He obviously has both knees pressed a little towards each other from the inside. The left side of his face is held to the right side of the golf ball. His

(Photo sequence from left to right)

Watson's stance is *wider* than his shoulders. Note left arm and club shaft continuity. Right elbow is *in* towards left, but not too much. He has an upright posture with the left side of his face aligned (just) to the right side of the golf ball.

His hands extend his arms back – the arms coil the shoulders.

His hips respond to his shoulder coil. There is a slight bend of his left knee as it begins its semicircular wind to the right – limited to the ball. The wrists are beginning to 'angle' (cock). There is no head shift. The left side of his face is still to the right side of the golf ball. Lateral extension is held – note retention to the left arm radius.

His left leg completes its semicircular wind. The right leg is still held into the left as it holds his body into the centre. Shoulders and hips are fully coiled – shoulders ninety degrees, hips forty-five degrees – on a vertically centralized axis. Head is still held just to right side of the ball.

The legs are the first to respond to the directional change of swing as his hands return forward, still constantly extended by a fixed left-arm radius.

The knees continue their leftward shuffle as hands and left arm move relentlessly forward to target (*think hands – think hands – not clubhead*).

There is a gradual counter-clockwise motion of the hands and left forearm . . .

. . . as swing approaches contact area or release.

stance is wide rather than narrow.

He extends back from target with no decreasing of left arm and shaft alignment. His trunk coils from hips to shoulders or shoulders to hips.

His right leg and foot hold his body into centre while his left foot is held as near to the ground as possible to supply resistance or tension to the coil.

He extends his hands and arms not only laterally but vertically high, making a near semicircle, orbiting in an upright tilt or plane in the space about him.

At the peak of his backswing he collected his 'optimum potential energy'.

The progression of sequence of movement in the down or forward swing is legs and hips, hands, arms, shoulders. His hands and arms have now transferred potential energy into kinetic energy. They are travelling at an ever-increasing speed, aided by his legs and his rotation, in the same plane as they went back, though, on a path a little behind that of the back swing. His head is held with the left side of his face still to the right side of the ball.

Impact or contact is influenced by the effect of centrifugal force, throwing the arms and club swing unit 'out and down', thus arching the wrists and the gradual but not violent counter-clockwise rotation of the hands and arms, which are simultaneously moving forward at an ever-increasing speed. There is no left wrist hinging, so the tendency would be to feel *the hands leading the clubhead past the ball*.

There is no collapse of the swing unit beyond contact as it extends parallel to target line, away from the swing centre.

It then moves vertically to complete the circle until . . .

... the speed is dissipated, into what I call a 'maypole' finish.

I am going to simplify the golf swing as we go along but it will be frequently necessary for you to refer to those common factors and how they relate to both the beginner and the experienced player.

There is no difference between men and women as far as method is concerned. There is only one golf swing but fourteen different clubs.

Let us now go to the ultimate in golf swing simplification – *The Wheel*. We shall be constantly referring to this throughout the book.

(Photo sequence from left to right)

The left arm gives a little, but only in preparation for . . .

. . . perfect contact extension, which under the influence of centrifugal force, arches a little and . . .

. . . through contact continues its gradual counter-clockwise wind, which is also matched by a similar wind of the left knee to the left. The head is still to the right of the ball position – left side of the face to the right side of the ball. The right foot has meanwhile been rolling onto the inside of the toe and the right knee closing into the left knee. There has been no relinquishing of the forward movement of the swing triangle. In fact from its shoulder base it has been *driving forward* in an accelerated 'for-ward drive' producing a clubhead speed of around 120 mph (193 kph). His hands and arms do not idle.

Extension visibly continues laterally to shoulder-high with the head only just beginning to rotate counter-clockwise while the hands and arms have virtually completed their counter-clockwise wind.

From lateral to vertical extension – from *out to up*!

A balanced maypole, which takes up the remaining energy. The right knee has reached the left knee. The back is gently arched in a reversed 'C'.

THE WHEEL

A study I have taken of the 'wheel golfer' should help you to get a skeleton picture of the ideal golf swing. The plane or tilt of the golf swing in particular is more clearly seen and understood. In the pictures opposite, top row, notice the differences of the tilt, angle or plane of the wheel rim. In the centre picture the wheel is upright because I put the *swing line board* below the base support at the back. In the first picture it is flat because the swing line board is below the front base support. In the top right picture it is neutral because the swing line board is away from the base support.

In the human swing wheel the plane is decided by the length of the club, the distance the ball is placed from the feet and the intentions of the player.

The path of the wheel golfer is easy to follow and like the human golfer is also much determined by the 'rotating hub' or the coiling human trunk. However, a birds-eye view of the wheel golfer can suggest that the path tracks parallel to the *target line* – see opposite centre picture. To a certain extent this is perfectly true. That it takes an 'inside to target line' path is purely due to hub turn. Certainly it has nothing to do with the spokes leaving the rim and tracking inside on their own. The spokes extend from centre to rim and are the wheel golfer's arc radius. The hands and arms do this for the human golfer.

When the wheel is turned back to the top it has collected enough *potential* energy to take it through to the equivalent distance on its forward swing, which is *kinetic* energy.

The wheel golfer does not have the joints and hinges nor hub size variations that seem to (but don't) turn the face of the club on the backswing, from square to out, or in golf jargon 'open'; note picture at nine o'clock on the imaginary clock behind the wheel facing the camera where the clubface position has apparently turned from square to open. Conversely,

at three o'clock on the forward swing, see picture opposite bottom right, the club-face has turned completely in the opposite direction until the back of the head, where the maker's name is, is pointing to the ball and the striking surface, the face of the club, looks at the imaginary clock. These are the human golfer's clubface effects. The wheel golfer's clubface would point down to the ground going back, and after contact, gradually up to the sky.

Through the contact or impact area the wheel golfer holds the clubface for 6 in (15.2 cm) before contact and 6 in after contact perfectly, along the swing-line board.

For the beginner it is the basic pattern to which the swinging movement should be moulded and even when the advanced stage is reached, should be constantly referred back to.

It must be remembered that all the instructions are written for right-handed players. Left-handed players do exactly the same, but substitute left for right on every occasion.

The wheel is really the perfect golfer: Below left, the front; below and bottom two side views with the 12-in (30.4 cm) *Target Line Board* suggesting *aim-position-posture-path-plane* and *swing arc*.

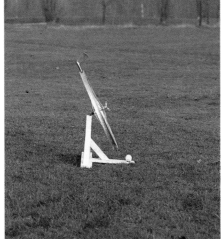

Above: Flat plane.
Above centre: Upright plane.
Above right: Normal plane.

The distance you stand away from the ball can also effect swing plane or tilt.

Right: Player's eye view suggests correct *feel* of hands path.
Bottom left: Halfway back – nine o'clock in the golf swing and the clubface is facing the photographer – this would be only in the human swing with all its complicated joints.
Bottom right: Halfway on the forward swing – three o'clock in the human swing and the clubface is looking away from the photographer.
Normally in the wheel swing the clubface at nine o'clock would point to the ground and at three o'clock it would point to the sky. You can't successfully play golf that way, though.

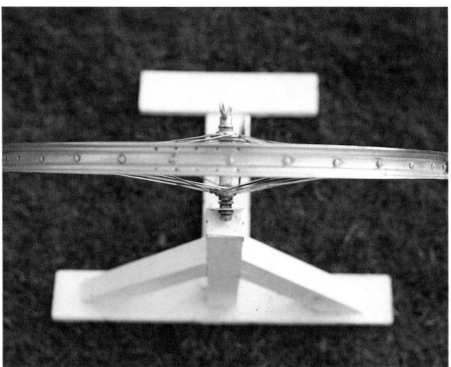

Aiming correctly is the first essential technique to playing a golf shot. When you have decided where you want your ball to land you must set yourself and your clubface in a position that will eliminate the least possibility of it going in another direction.

Aiming correctly is no guarantee that the ball will go in the direction you want it to go, but if you swing well and yet aim wrongly, you have only yourself to blame when the ball flies off at an unintended tangent.

As a teacher I am constantly checking for aim. Too often in my experience incorrect aiming is more the effect of not bothering to make an aim routine because it is 'only on the practice ground'. Students who will actually admit to this type of mental and physical indolence, can only be as slipshod on the course. It has got to matter that you take aim whether you are playing or practising.

On the practice ground at Birkdale during the 1983 Open, Jack Nicklaus was checking and double checking with his caddie that he was correctly lined up with his shoulders. This is an important aspect of aiming and quite a number of professionals will place a club on the ground pointing in the direction of their target to use as a guide. I have seen Bob Byman, of the USA, Scandinavian Open Champion for 1982, using two clubs with which to aim and align himself.

There is more to be gained from aiming correctly than the reduction of off-target shots through incorrect aiming. For example, you are establishing a line – call it the target line – along which, not only do you want the ball to fly, but along which you have established a line to swing.

You will not actually swing along that line for the whole of the swing and the clubhead may at best travel only 12 in (30.4 cm) along it: 6 in (15.2 cm) through contact, and possibly 6 in at the start of

the backswing. However, your hands should stay parallel to it for some considerable time after that. The target line you must establish is an absolutely necessary physical and mental guide to the path along which you are going to track your swing.

You are doing something else when you take aim. You are telling that part of your reflex system that controls movement that you are about to play a golf shot. So, it will not be taken by surprise: your computer has been programmed; you have conditioned your reflexes; and conditioned reflexes react much more effectively than those 'taken by surprise'.

There was a specific aim routine taught by the American Professional Golfers' Association teaching school at Palm Beach Shores, Florida in 1972. I have taught it ever since because I believe it is the best way to do it.

It is mere guesswork to stand in a playing position and try to aim from there. There's perhaps a touch of laziness, too, with an 'it can't be as important as that', attitude, thrown in. You can best make or find your target line from a position behind the ball so that the ball is between you and your target. It may be a tree, a post, a pylon, the horizon, or the flagstick or any such prominent object in the direction you have decided to land the golf ball.

Holding the club in your right hand, if you are right-handed, and in your left if you are left-handed (the American PGA school insisted that their students, and some were tour players, should use only the right hand during their stay at the school and for very good reasons as you will eventually see) draw an imaginary line from your target down to the golf ball. That is your *Target Line*. Now, pick a spot on that line, this would be any irregularity on the surface of the ground such as a weed, an old divot mark (which shouldn't really be there if etiquette had been

properly observed) even a darker or lighter shade of grass, about 2 ft (609 mm) away from the ball. This spot becomes your target – your *intermediate target*. It is much easier now to set the face of your club (the striking surface) to the nearer target and therefore easier to aim than using the ultimate distant one.

The next time you watch Jack Nicklaus driving from the tee, you will realize that he pays a lot of attention to his intermediate target before he begins to swing. As I said earlier, Nicklaus is quite obsessive about aim and his checking and counter-checking is probably one of the many reasons for his domination of the golfing world.

You have established your target and your intermediate target. Place the clubhead, still holding the club in your right hand only, behind the ball, that is, in a striking position (see photo **2**) with the face 'square to the spot' or more accurately, at right angles to that target line. While you are doing this, your feet should be fairly close together with the left foot in line with the ball and slightly drawn back up to 2 in (5 cm) from the right foot. In golfing terms, a slightly 'open stance'.

You will be impatient by now and itching to get on with the rest of it. I want you to break off from your aimed clubface position and go through that same routine all over again.

1. Stand behind the ball.

2. Holding the club with the right hand only, draw the line from target to ball.
3. Pick a spot 2 ft (609 mm) approximately on that line in front of the ball.
4. With feet near together – ball opposite your left toe and stance slightly open, set the face of the club to the near target.

With this slightly open aiming stance, and holding with your right hand only, you will have (a), a better view of your target and (b), it will be easier to align your shoulders, which should be square to the target line.

If you use your left hand only with which to aim, you are very likely to end up standing 'closed' to your target and therefore aiming to the right. Keep the clubhead grounded as you grip.

'Aiming' photos show the four-part routine.
Top row: On target to ball line – fix your intermediate target.
Square your clubface behind ball to your intermediate target.
Take your grip.
Take your stance.
Middle and bottom rows: The two Club golfers nearly get it right. A little more practice and they will be as precise as the professionals – who are all different but all look the same.
The lady has forgotten to look at her target before starting her backswing. This would have helped to mirror on her mind the path her forward swing should take. The man has probably taken his grip and stance at the same time. This could be to the detriment of one or the other or both. Aim, grip, stance, posture, visual target check, should be embarked upon separately.

You have taken aim and grip. However, the golf grip is so specific, even if it does have a few tolerances, that it needs the next chapter all to itself. Meanwhile we will carry on with the completion of the routine, while you take a temporary grip.

Widen your feet, right foot first and this should be placed at right angles to your target line. Assuming you are using a driver, (the longest club for the longest shot) the left heel should be opposite the ball and the toe turned out forty-five degrees. Both toes should be in line, and that line should be parallel to the target line. There is an allowable tolerance for the left foot to be drawn back a shade up to, but no more than 2 in (5 cm). I have yet to find any real general advantage in a 'closed' stance, that is, with the left foot advanced up to 2 in (5 cm). In fact, this tends to be a disadvantage for a number of reasons. Having said that, it could be used

The pros all have similar common factors. They stand a little more over the ball, however, than the description 'upright' would suggest. The opposite to upright would really be 'on all fours', that is, both hands and feet on the ground: but in the case of the golf-swing posture it is meant to describe the opposite to 'slumping' with slouched shoulders and chin sunk into chest. The bend is more from the waist. There is no floppiness. They are all muscularly alert. All the stances are comfortably wide with the right toe at right angles to the target line and the left toe turned out to target about forty-five degrees. The left foot varies a little from being in line with the right toe to being slightly – less than 2 in (5 cm) – drawn back from it. Pressures are mainly in towards each other at the feet and the same at the knees.

The front views show a left-arm shaft continuity while the side views show a slightly dropped wrist angle. The ball positions vary from centre to left heel with irons and woods respectively.

Gordon Brand jnr., M. Kuramoto, V. Somers, Lanny Wadkins, Gary Koch, Tom Kite, Simon Hobday, Hale Irwin, Bobby Clampett, Larry Nelson, Hal Sutton, and David Graham demonstrate perfect head centring and even distribution of pressure between both feet. The lady is showing a preponderance of leftward pressure while the junior player has his head leaning right. Ideally, it should be centred in line with the ball, but it can be *rotated* slightly to the right. Stance width for a driver should be as wide as your shoulders measured from the *insides* of your feet.

to help the very portly to turn more on the backswing, but then there would be the vexed problem of returning.

Your stance should be wide rather than narrow. Perhaps the only concession to comfort I shall concede will be that your stance should be 'comfortably wide', but certainly not comfortably narrow. A wide stance – square – or slightly open to target line, is a superstar common factor.

There are a few advantages derived from a wide stance, one not so widely realized is that you can generate more swing speed with those feet well apart than when they are nearer together. The plank theory goes: You will walk more spritely over a wide plank across a deep chasm than you would a narrow one!

Another disadvantage of a narrow stance is the risk of committing the most feared fault on the professional circuit, 'coming over the top'. In simplest terms, this means returning the swing on a path

that tracks first outside the target line and then inside it. It produces anything from a bad hook (which curves to the left rather abruptly) to a pulled slice (where the ball goes straight to the left, then curves to the right). The wide stance is quite a good insurance against the financial losses involved when this fault, known as 'tour terror' takes over.

You have lined up with your clubface and your feet. Your shoulders should now be turned into position parallel to the target line, and here is where so many golfers go wrong. They point the left shoulder to the ultimate target, which means that they end up pointing diagonally to the right of the target line and they are immediately aiming off to the right. I would remind you that your arms are attached to your shoulders and so they are considerably influenced by the shoulders' orientation.

You should intend to take your swing with your hands and arms mainly in a parallel to the target line path. You are jeopardizing the possibility of this by starting off with your shoulders pointing to the right, or to the left.

You are aimed. However, there are seven loose threads to be tied up before you are completely assembled for action:

1. Your posture should be 'up' rather than slouched, but this must not be interpreted as standing to attention. The length of the club you are using will influence your waist angle, which will in turn effect your spinal angle.

2. You should have some pressure exerted from the insides of your knees and along the insides of both feet. In the former you will feel a little knock-kneed. In the latter you will feel as if you are clawing the ground with your toes, but don't be averse to feeling some pressure to your heels. *Pressure is defined as the force acting normally per unit area.*

3. Your weight distribution should be fairly equally spread between both feet at the golf swing assembly or address. *The weight of a body is the force it exerts on anything which supports it.*

4. Ideally your hip platform should be turned slightly to the left.

5. Your head while remaining central to your feet, could be *rotated*, without losing its centre, slightly to the right, so that the left side of your face is just to the right side of the golf ball.

6. Check that your left arm and club shaft are held in a continuous line but with your wrists slightly sunk.

7. This brings us to another superstar check: The distance of your hands away from you. The length of the club will determine the distance the ball is away from your feet – that is as variable as the lengths of the clubs are. There is little variation between the positions of the ball in relation to your feet. If you play the

Top left: A brilliant young amateur player has a correct left-arm club line with sufficient wrist sinkage. The heel of his left hand is held the required 6 in (15.2 cm) from his left thigh. Note Lee Trevino (above centre) P. Oosterhuis (above right) and Brian Waites (right) similarly place their hands. Left: The lady's wrists are slightly arched. The spinal angle varies with the length of the club.

with the ball opposite the centre of your feet, the longer irons from 5 to 1 between centre and left heel, and your woods opposite your left heel, you will be on very safe ground.

I shall mention any differences as they may arise in the special shots. Too many players extend their arms to the ball, at assembly so much that far too much weight is put on their toes. Unfortunately, it always seems more powerful to get down to it but this is sheer illusion and only deprives you of that very body balance which is so essential to power. It produces a very flat plane and the clubhead is tracked for only the minimum time along the target line.

When your hands are positioned nearer to you the swing plane is more *upright* and this helps to ensure that the path of the clubhead will stay the maximum time along the target line. This is a decided

When you sink your wrists a little, you not only bring your hand unit nearer to your left leg, but you are accommodating the arching effect on your wrists, which is the reaction of centrifugal force through contact.

If your hands are more than 6 in (15.2 cm) away from your left thigh when you do sink your wrists a little, the gap should be narrowed to 6 in (15.2 cm) by shuffling your feet forwards as much as is necessary to effect that distance. Obviously, the measurement will be taken from that part of your left hand that is nearest to your left leg.

There may be physical reasons why you can't get so near and 1 in (2.5 cm) tolerances either way can be acceptable. However, *none* of these should include 'Because it feels too awkward'.

I have nought for your comfort as you turn to the next chapter on the grip.

Peter Jacobsen (below left), Severiano Ballesteros (below), Greg Norman (bottom left) show all the correct common factors. They are bristling with obvious muscular alertness, like runners about to spring at the starter's pistol.

One of the advantages of aiming with the club in your right hand only is that you will be able to assemble the grip with your right hand already on the shaft. You have merely to slot your left hand into your right hand.

In my experience as a teacher I have found that the majority of beginners have the utmost difficulty in placing their right hand on the shaft correctly when the left hand is already there. But, when I ask them to hold the club with the right hand only, they place it in exactly the right position.

If you have no difficulty in positioning your right hand correctly with the left hand already on the grip, it is completely acceptable to take your grip with the left hand first. Many superstars do this.

It is most important to have the right hand holding in a specific way. This should be the position it arrives at on contact. From your eye view this would mean the first joint of the forefinger, the joint furthest away from the finger nail, pointing directly to the ground, or at right angles to the ground.

When the right hand is placed *under* the shaft with the forefinger pointing to the left foot, it automatically rights itself during the swing and comes back to contact correctly. Alas, it ignores the clubface which, because of this spontaneous correction, points to the left on contact.

Conversely, when the right hand is held too far to the left of the grip with the forefinger pointing to the right foot, the correction leaves the clubface pointing to the right on contact.

The right-hand grip should be held more to the tips of the fingers so that the palm can wrap over the left thumb as much as possible.

It could therefore be said with some validity that *the major role of the right hand is in controlling the face of the club.* It has a minor role in supporting the left hand and a general one of being a part of the hands or grip unit. *It should be a constant.*

The pressure point of the right hand is located in the forefinger and thumb area and it is directed upwards towards the base of the left thumb. The pressure should be firm, the grip neither tight nor loose.

Slotting the left hand into the right hand involves mainly the thumb and forefinger of this hand. The thumb fits snugly into the hollow of the right palm just below the base of the right thumb. The forefinger is either overlapped by, or interlocked with, the little finger of the right hand.

The choice is yours: Overlapping the left forefinger or interlocking it with the little finger, it is equally effective in assisting manual unity. The majority of superstars overlap. Interlocking the left forefinger with the little finger of the right hand has held Jack Nicklaus in good stead throughout his uniquely magnificent

The right hand grips with emphasis on the first joint of the forefinger held at right angles to the ground. If it starts here it will most likely be in this position through contact.

The club is correctly held across the finger tips.

The sixth left hand finger: the palm pad with the grip wedged between this and the little finger.

career! *The left hand's major role is to weld the club to you.* It has six fingers, if you count the fleshy pad at the base of the hand nearest to the wrist below the little finger as a finger, and count the thumb as a finger like the Swedes do. The shaft should fit more to the base of the fingers and be wedged below that palm pad.

The left-hand pressure is on the last three fingers, those nearest to you. This pressure is in a counter-clockwise direction and down, as though you are pulling a glove onto this hand with the right hand from the back. As with the right hand the pressure is firm but not tight, certainly not loose.

The left hand is a variable. You can twist it round to casually glance down at the back of it so you can see three knuckles. You shouldn't have it so far round that you can see four knuckles. You can have it round a little less to the right so that you can see only two. Seeing one knuckle only is a very weak position and far more superstars use a well-wrapped-round left hand showing two to three knuckles than is popularly supposed.

One thing is certain, you will experience awkwardness and a right hand weakness at first with the correct grip, but with patience and perseverance this awkwardness and weak feeling will disappear. The long-term effects will be well worth your application.

Gripping with your palms always 'feels' strong. I cannot stress too much the value of cultivating a fingers' hold with your palms wrapped round rather than the reverse.

When you are assembled with your grip, stance, posture, and pressure formula completed, you have made sixty percent of your golf swing. Yes, sixty percent, and all of this is static!

You can practise this anywhere. Even indoors without any danger of damaging chandeliers, furniture, windows, walls or doors. You can even practise your grip, one hand and two hands while you are sitting comfortably in your armchair watching television.

Regardless of where you practise, even only for a few minutes a day, say a minimum of thirty, you *must* practise

The complete grip. Note the trigger hold of the right forefinger and thumb. The left thumb should never be far enough down the shaft to prize open this trigger.

Approach the shaft with the left hand from the right side of the shaft . . .

. . . and with the right hand from the left side. In both cases, note that the palms are orientated to the ground. By doing it this way you will get a better finger grip and 'palm-wrap'.

The *Vardon grip*: Right little finger rests on the knuckle of the left forefinger.

The *overlock*: Right little finger secured behind the knuckles of the left forefinger.

The *interlocking*: Right little finger and left forefinger entwined. The original interlocking grip invented by Alex Morison in the thirties had the left thumb 'outside' the right hand and touching the left forefinger.

ON THE WAY

When you are completely assembled in the static with your grip, stance, posture and pressure formula, and about to start the dynamic part of the swing you will experience some muscular tension. As long as it does not involve extreme tightness of the muscles this condition should be cultivated.

Tension being a variable, you should aim for the alertness and springiness, of a runner awaiting the starter's pistol.

You should not be muscularly relaxed. You should exert a little pressure on the last three left-hand fingers before starting, and there is a lot to be said for making a little wave of your hands, in golfing parlance, a 'waggle', back and forth, on what would be your intended swing path. I am not going to enlarge on that wave. Most superstars have some preliminary movement that *appears* to be superficial. Even a leftward flex of the right knee like Gary Player for example, which is known as a *forward press* has some meaning in the context of the whole movement. If a wave or waggle and a forward press effectively reduces extreme tension to feasible and necessary tension then, by all means adopt this introduction to your swing. A warning, though, it can be counter-productive if you do too much of it or take too long over it. You will come out of your assembly position before you have even begun to swing.

When we turn the wheel back what happens? The hub turns on its axis. The rim turns in perfect path and plane. The radius remains constant. The base stays firm.

Transcribe that movement to the human frame and it goes as follows. The arms initiate the movement via the hands, which turn, twist or coil the trunk. The base is held from feet to knees (and knees to feet) and held in centre by the head and right leg. The path and plane are allied to the start angle of the spine, the target line and the trunk rotation.

If you look at the photo opposite top right, the player's eye view of the wheel, you will see that this perspective appears to make the wheel rim parallel to the target line. It is therefore quite conceivable that the swing path and plane are related to the target line and should follow a parallel to the target line path away from the target. The plane and path are also related to the trunk rotation, and the plane to the lie and length of the club.

You must remember that the wheel has only one moveable joint – at the hub. The human body has in the region of two hundred moveable joints, which obviously make the human golf swing more complicated.

As the backswing progresses the effects of inertia and continuity will try to force the wrists and the right elbow to bend. I say try because these effects of the laws of physics can be too easily inhibited by the human computer. The trick is to *allow* flexibility where it should occur. For instance keep the wrist flex to the base of the thumbs (this is the acceptable pivotal point of the wrists), and the right elbow flex in a down-to-the-ground direction, rather than up to the sky. The left arm should be kept as extended at the elbow joint as is tolerable, to maintain the radius.

The back of the left hand should be as continuous as is tolerable with the left wrist.

A good check for plane is to swing back to half way – about hip high – and then turn your feet at right angles. You are now facing what was your right side view. Your arms should be extended directly from you and when you place the club on the ground you should be in a perfect start position, but of course aiming at right angles to your original position – see photos at bottom right of these two pages. If your path has been increasingly too far *inside* the target line, your check position will place the club opposite your right

One thing the superstars have in common is that they coil, virtually from the knees up to the shoulders. They stay so much on a centre that they could well be encased in a tube. Only their arms extend away from their rotating trunk while their feet and legs support and resist the body turn. I say the arms extend away from the body in the context of not contracting into the body. So many beginners and handicap players are afraid to allow their arms to keep their distance from the body centre. The path of the swing back is directly away from the target but the trunk turn orbits this path increasingly 'inside', but parallel to, the target line as the back swing progresses.

If the amateur lady and pro Simon Hobday were to check their swing plane like the 16-year-old in the bottom row photographs there could be no doubt that they would find themselves correctly planed.

foot. If your path has been increasingly *outside* the target line you will ground your club opposite your left foot.

There should be no weight shift on the backswing, only a slight change of pressure on the left foot from all along the inside of the foot to inside the ball of the foot. The right foot pressure should remain as it started – all along the inside of the foot.

The backswing continues at a leisurely pace *out* and *up* but, as it progresses, the legs supporting the trunk turn, take more and more strain until they can no longer retain their position and are compelled to flex leftwards, target direction, to initiate the *return* or *forward swing*. The shoulders will have coiled in the region of ninety degrees and the hips in the region of forty-five degrees.

You can't measure this but you should be looking at the ball over the tip of your left shoulder as your hands and arms

All these top players have the back of their left hand in line, no matter what the plane of the swing is. Notice also how the right leg holds into the centre by staying more or less where it started. For the most part they tend to have high back swings. Also, they have the left shoulder turned far enough to be in line with the golf ball. Lanny Wadkins is an exception, perhaps, but nevertheless he does make an approachable coil. The front of the left knee in every case 'looks at the ball' which helps tighten the spring and reduce the hip turn to half that of the shoulders. The amateur (right) compares well with Wadkins (below) and Kuramoto (bottom), except that his knee is a little more extended than theirs at the top of the backswing. Note also the other amateurs (opposite top) and Gordon Brand jnr. (opposite centre).

reach the backswing summit and the legs strain, particularly in the flexed (to the left) to right leg should indicate that the hips have reached their optimum twist.

To abbreviate this down to Irv Schloss's verbal economy, 'You stretch your arms against your knees away from the target and rotate on centre'. Described by author and journalist John Reece as 'a flat-footed twist', it is in fact not all that flat-footed either. It is not at all uncommon for the left heel to leave the ground on the backswing. It is actually a common factor amongst the superstars to have the left heel off the ground. This will vary from a half (1.25 cm) to 1 in (2.5 cm). More than 1 in would dissipate the necessary tension of the coil and result in loss of elasticity and centre. For the more portly player who would find coiling physically difficult, optimum left heel elevation would give him his optimum turn. The slimmer figure might need to keep the left heel on the ground. In all cases of physical limitations you must remember that if you are doing as much as you can (although not achieving as much as you would like!), as long as you are moving within your *tolerances*, you are in effect doing what you should.

The backswing is all very much like the pull of elastic in a catapult while the handle (which comprises the legs below the knees, and the feet) is held.

You have collected optimum *potential* energy which, on the forward swing, will be turned into *kinetic* energy.

Your legs should be on the way to target even now.

Just as you *turn* on the backswing you *return* on the forward swing. The only difference is in the sequence of the turning.

Greg Norman (opposite top) and Peter Oosterhuis (opposite centre) coil correctly and extend their arms, via their hands, sideways and upwards with no loss of vertical width. Oosterhuis's shortness in upward stretch is compensated for by his bodily height. Bobby Clampett's (bottom row opposite) left hand and wrist line in centre picture are maintained as he makes his backswing summit. The turn against the legs is demonstrated. His right elbow points to the ground. He is ready to change direction and return in sequence.

Tom Kite (top row) is in perfect conformity for return committal. Ballesteros (left) stretches and turns with his legs held 'in'. Gary Koch (bottom row), lean and lithe, turns on centre.

There are no outrageously high left heels and no outrageously high-to-the-sky right elbows. This is important because if you lift the left heel too high you will be altering your *start waist angle* and this means lifting your head and your body, which alters the plane and the path of your swing. Ray Floyd lifts his left heel on the backswing more than most but he bends his left knee more to the ball and thus neutralizes the possibility of a body lift.

A high-to-the-sky right elbow could cause an excessive dip of the waist angle and again affect the plane and path of the swing.

You will notice with all the tour pros that the hips have coiled rather more than is popularly supposed.

It is rare to see a superstar or even any tour player with a really short backswing. In fact, most of them share the common factor of having quite long backswings. By long, I mean the shaft of the club at the top of the swing is parallel to the ground

or even in some cases below the parallel. There are, for instance, more tour players with swings below the parallel than above it.

What is apparent, however, is the effect of ageing, when a shortening of the backswing arms extension, and to a relative extent a shortening of the coil (this is not so visible), occurs.

There is nothing conscious about this. The player does not decide to shorten his swing because he has just celebrated his forty-seventh or his fifty-seventh birthday. The ageing process decides this for him. As far as he is concerned, the backswing will feel just as it always did.

The important point I am making here is, do not *try* to shorten your backswing. *Extend back sideways and upwards with your arms and coil on centre from above the knees up to your shoulders within your tolerance, at a pace that allows you the best control.*

All photos are of amateur students of mine.

FORWARD SWING

One of the difficulties about the golf swing is its deception of feel and the many interpretations of the sequence of movement. You can, for instance, 'feel' you are making a certain movement and yet not be. If a movement feels 'comfortable' it will most likely be an incorrect one. It is possible to say, and be right, that the legs start off the change of direction sequence. It is possible to say that the hips do this, and be right. It is possible to say that the hands initiate directional change, and be right. One school of thought will say the shoulders tilt. The left shoulder goes up and the right one goes down to initiate the return movement.

All these views are valid when looked at in the context of a player's *key*, which activates all the other parts of the whole movement. For instance, if player 'A' feels that he/she starts the 'return' swing, or 'downswing' from the top of the backswing into directional change with his legs, this does not necessarily mean that he actually does start with his legs. It could mean that he starts with his hands but he

has to feel the movement initiated in his legs to 'allow' his hands to change direction.

Look at the Watson sequence again and the twenty superstars on the ensuing pages. At the top of the backswing the legs are wound above the knees against the lower legs and feet. On any photo of the return swing this situation has changed dramatically. It is as though both knees, the left in particular, have released themselves from the backswing tension and have sprung to the left in the target direction.

In many of the superstars – look at the Palmer sequence – the stress of the backswing body coil on the legs has made the situation untenable for them and the left knee is moving out of this spring even *before* the backswing (with the hands and arms) has been completed. Nevertheless this does not *hasten* the directional change of the hands. They are still tracking back and collecting an enormous amount of potential energy. This movement must be unhurried.

This is aided and abetted by the already reversing legs and hips. I have delayed introducing the hip platform until now because the spontaneous shuffle of the legs has already involved the hip platform to which they are attached. You will probably see how the snowballing effect of this integrated sequence of parts related to the whole movement, complement each other. What is more, any one part correctly made will automatically trigger off a chain reaction throughout the whole movement.

You will appreciate from this the importance of not only knowing the parts, but also practising those part movements and then linking them to the whole movement.

Because of the deception of feel in movement it is possible to be making a fault in a part without realizing it. This is why coaching or teaching is so important. It is very difficult and in some cases impossible to detect a faulty part in your own swing. Obviously, if you know more about the parts and the whole movement,

M. Kuramoto (left), the lady amateur (top) and Gordon Brand jnr. (above) have changed swing direction with hands and legs. It is noticeable that the hands and knees work in co-ordination and the hips are also activated. The shoulders follow in sequence. There should be no undue delay of the shoulders as they follow legs and lower body to the swing finish.

you have a better chance of analyzing yourself.

Faults are the outcome of the reflex system that governs movement, resorting to comfort on the one hand, and the effects of trying to hit too hard or not hard enough (quitting) under the pressures of the game, on the other. Unfortunately, faults will make their own chain reactions, which cut across the normal ones. Rather like weeds appearing on the greens.

The directional change of the swing is a very critical part of the swing. You will certainly have less to worry about if your backswing is good but your chances are considerably reduced if a fault or faults have crept in there.

That wrist angle you collected on the backswing should be retained. If you didn't collect backwards, you must do so on forward swing.

There is no doubt that the sequence is: legs, hands and then arms. There should be some delay of the shoulders. Too many golfers, even experienced ones, start the return swing with a shoulder rotation. The head position is affected by the shoulders but the head can also help to delay the shoulders and thus hold them in sequence. It sounds easy enough to keep the left side of your face to the right side of the ball until the ball has gone but psychological pressures can make this simple positioning quite difficult. Eventually you will find you have got to discipline yourself until the habit is formed.

Legs, hands, arms and head control are involved as you rapidly come into the contact area. In fact, the whole of the forward movement increases pace as it progresses and occupies only a little over one second in time to complete. *Once you are committed to the return swing you are committed to the end of the swing.* It is then really too late to change your mind. *Part learning* is only for the practice ground.

The directional change of the swing is not practised nearly as much as it should be. This is mainly because once the swing has begun to roller-coast downhill from the top, it is rather difficult to stop. It should therefore be practised at slow-motion pace and stopped around hip-high level. Hands and arms, knees and hips sliding to the left with the wrist angle maintained and the hands 'separating from the shoulders – or, in other words, the distance of the hands from the shoulders at the top of the backswing increasing as the down swing, or as I prefer to call it, the forward swing, progresses.

Try that again. Hands move down from shoulders and the original gap between them widens the further the swing goes. The knees bend to the left and cause the hips to slide sideways to the left, coupled with a slight raising of the right heel in towards the left and the right foot is beginning to transfer weight to the left foot.

If you think you are working hard at this, let me tell you about the time I watched Gary Player for over three hours repeating this movement. During a practice game for the 'Open' at St Andrews in 1960, three colleagues and myself walked off the seventeenth green to play the last hole. Gary was on the tee intensely repeating from the top of his backswing to hip high, and then back again. He missed no step as he established the habit: legs, hips, hands – hands, hips, legs. He kept his wrists angled, that is, he retained the wrist angle he had collected on the backswing, and his left arm radius extended. His right elbow dug into his right side. His right heel elevated in towards his left heel as he rolled onto the inside of the toe of the right shoe. His head remained centred with his left cheek at right angles to the ground positioned just to the right of that golf ball. He went through all this over and over again without even noticing us. It was 7.30 pm when we arrived at the tee. It was dark and 10.30 pm when he concluded his practice. We never did play the last hole of that practice game but at least we were given an object lesson in dedication.

Let us continue through contact. Unless, of course, you are too busy perfecting that initial directional change movement. If you are, please remember to use your legs by pushing your knees to your target as well as pulling your hands. Your knees will connect energy to your hands.

Pictures on this and opposite page are all of amateur students of mine who know how to maintain the wrist angle, in other words, not to hit *at* the ball, but to take the swing through to its conclusion continuously with the legs leading the body return. In each case the head controls centre with the left side of the face held to the right side of the ball until the ball has gone. The change of direction like the concluding of the backswing *should not be hurried*, though you need not be deliberately slow. On the backswing the left knee makes a semicircle to the right, completing itself when the left knee points to the golf ball or thereabouts. On the return swing the left knee retraces this semicircle back to an extended position. The right knee should have closed the gap between the knees.

FORWARD SWING

Lanny Wadkins (left) and Larry Nelson (below) from top of backswing to contact. You must remember that these two positions are segments of a whole movement that are excellent frozen actions but which form an active, dynamic irresistible flow of kinetic energy that continues until the energy is dissipated. You can't stop to check, you can't stop to think. Once you have embarked on the return swing you are committed until it is finished. Wadkins on contact or release shows the effect of centrifugal force extending the cocked wrists. The counter-clockwise rotation of forearms and body transmit this to the clubhead – if you let it – as it breaks through the resistance of the ball. Continuity is essential to regain momentum and acceleration, which has suffered a fleeting loss of this while breaking through resistance.

The retention of David Graham's wrist angle is clearly seen (right), but (far right) much of its gradual loss comes from the counter-clockwise rotation of his body from feet to shoulders. Larry Nelson (below) is clearly holding on to his wrist-angle retention. His hands are beyond (to the left of) the ball before his clubface has connected with it. This is literally squeezing the ball off the ground.

Contact Area

The contact area begins approximately about hip high on the down swing to above hip high on the follow through – or from hands at right hip level to hands at left hip level. Within this area you should be actively engaged in keeping on centre and maintaining hands/arms movement so that the clubhead travels along or just inside a broad white line 12 in (30.4 cm) in length, for 6 in (15.2 cm) before the golf ball and 6 in after it, at a speed that increases as the swing progresses. The former is achieved mainly by keeping your left cheek to the right side of the ball until the ball has gone. But there are other ingredients that help to make good centring. The hips, for example, rotating in a counter-clockwise direction help to hold a body centre. These are assisted by a responsive leg action, which also transfers whatever body weight is on the right foot to the left foot, and this is another factor that contributes to centring and balance. There could not be a wheel without a centrally rotating hub. The trunk supported by the legs is the *hub* of the golf swing wheel.

There could not be a wheel without spokes or *radii*. The left arm is the golf-swing radius. This lynch-pin *must* be extended, braced, locked or just firm at the elbow joint, through the contact area but if deviation of this occurs before or after contact, and it shouldn't, there is little or no tolerance here for a left-arm collapse of any dimension.

At this stage I must remind you that we are talking about a swing part or segment taken from the whole movement. The contact area takes around seven sixty-fourths of a second to complete. It is absolutely outside the capabilities of any human being to think of the movements involved in this area and simultaneously consciously try to perform them.

It is possible to take one part of this segment, for example, the raising of the right heel, and concentrate on this while the swing is allowed to continue without hinder. You will need to repeat this right heel 'pedestal' movement for a few weeks until it begins to respond itself to the earlier positions and movements and to the ensuing ones. Remember Gary Player and his 'directional-change' practice! Once it becomes a habit you can switch to another emphasis. You will know when the time is ripe for a change of emphasis. The link between your right foot and the knee (which is also involved) and the reflex system, will pre-empt your thought process.

Youthful prodigy Barry Winton is seen skilfully demonstrating: (1) The right foot pedestal where the right heel rises towards the left heel. It rolls onto the inside of the toe, thus transferring the weight to the left side. Note his retention of wrist angle (above and above right). (2) The clubhead travels along the 12 in (30.4 cm) white line (right). This is the main key to co-ordination in golf, *hands-eye-clubhead*-and-*ball* linkage to clinch contact perfection. Note the arching of wrist-hand line, the effect of the reaction of centrifugal force. But remember, the time spreading through contact is so fleeting that the human eye cannot register it. The 12-in white line is the one thing you should take onto the course with you. You just cannot go equipped with the overwhelming burden of multiple swing parts clogging your muscle memory. With all your shots you need your selected club, target area and your mental 12-in white line. Your swing should be quite habitual, back and through, and your rhythm as controlled as your temper. Only look for the result *after* the ball has gone and look in the direction of your target where you want the ball to go.

Now I am going to draw you to a halt before taking you through contact to the end of the swing because I want you to get a 'live' feel of this, the most critical segment of the whole movement.

Get hold of a golf club. If you have a choice, a wedge, or a 9-iron, or better still a putter. If not, any golf club will do, or even a short broom handle.

Take your grip and stance. Remember, an even spread of pressure between both feet along the insides, and also the insides of both knees, but please, don't exaggerate the latter. Swing back and forth with your hands and arms extending back just past your right knee and forward just past your left knee. Keep your arms straight, especially the left. You are *scooping*. I want you to *scrape* the mat, but refrain from taking divots! They don't replace as easily as they will on the course. Scraping means your hands and arms *pull* the clubhead or the broom head through the ball position. You have no ball there. At least you shouldn't have, or the TV set, the china cabinet and the cat will be directly imperilled, perhaps even your marriage.

Keep the pendulum flowing. Back and forth. Increase it a little to nearly half way back, that would be to eight o'clock on the clock behind you from the six o'clock start and through to four o'clock. It's just

hands and arms back. Scrape forward, scrape at six o'clock continuously to four o'clock. Do it again and again. A slight flex of the right knee as you scrape forward helps the flow of movement. You may even feel the wrists flexing a little on the backswing, but they shouldn't unflex on the way forward. If there were a ball there, there would be no need to *hit at* it. It would stay there until the clubhead met it, during the continuity of the swing, that is if you are standing the right distance away from the ball and you are staying on a steady centre.

Before you take the swing back to nine o'clock and then forward to three o'clock, still scraping the carpet (gently) at six o'clock where the ball would be in a real shot, check you have enough room to swing back to nine, and forward to three, scrape at six; scrape along that 12 in (30.4 cm) white line. Bend the right knee a bit towards the left knee, you may even raise your right heel a little in towards your left heel. Back and forth. You will feel a rhythm. *One and two*, and a slight shift of weight to your left foot as you go through to three, but the centre stays intact.

These should be your first shots on the practice ground: Seven to five, eight to four, and nine to three. *Graduate* to the big shots with the big swing. We will go back to that big swing now, and a little more

This exercise is really the big swing in miniature. I am demonstrating here the simple movement back from, and forward movement to, the target with my hands. I am not flipping, flicking, scooping or shoving with my hands. I am using them to: (1) hold the club and (2) propel my arms in the two directions on an intended path and at an intended length to which the speed of this movement is related. I am doing nothing to add to or to take away from this swing flow as I take my hands through the location of the golf ball. In every case, I am *not hitting at the ball*, it merely gets in the way of the face of my club to which it readily responds so long as my hands and arms keep moving through the resistance in that ball. I let the length of the swing determine the speed of the swing, neither adding to nor subtracting from the spontaneous momentum. The temptation to make a hit is nearly too much, but this is where discipline, like practice, is so essential.

My demonstration on these two pages is to emphasize the strength of two hands united as one. Neither in the example of the flick nor the forward drive have I used my legs. Use of legs transmits more energy to the unitized hands swing. The flick short-circuits any transmission of energy as the hands and wrists work independently.

detail of the contact area you have been putting into movement practice. Remember you are learning a movement when you are learning to play golf. It has shape and pace.

The wrist angle retention need not consciously be released. It happens by the spontaneous reaction of centrifugal force. This force acting outwards and downwards, arches the wrists and lifts the heel of the golf club, so that the toe of the club

tends to travel nearer the ground than the heel through contact.

This phenomenon was discovered many years ago by two USA professionals, researching on the golf swing. It was noticed by Frank Walsh and Al Watrous that the divot marks on the par three tees, during a major professional event, were higher nearer the player, and deeper further out. The toes of the iron clubs the pros used on these tees had, in other words, dug more deeply than the heels. This was clearly the effect of centrifugal force.

As the return swing continues forward to target, the forearms should wind progressively counterclockwise. Try to feel this rotation with the left forearm. If you can exercise more control with the left arm and your left side you will have fewer flight errors to correct. Ideally, use two hands as one unit.

It is worth recording that all the advocates of hitting hard with the right hand do qualify this by advising an unbroken, firm left wrist and arm (in other words, the elbow joint).

In my 'bucket of balls' pictures (pages 56–57) I am flicking at the bucket from a static position, trying to knock it over. In the first picture I could have flicked all day and made no impression. In the next pictures I am 'pulling' from the static, that is, both hands and forearms are driving forwards, the clubhead *has* to follow and the power thus generated immediately tips the bucket over.

The pull, the scrape or the forward-to-target drive of the hands and arms with the left arm firm and predominant is a common factor of every superstar.

You see, it doesn't really matter about that right hand hit as long as the left is not neutralized or negated by it. A collapsed left elbow and wrist is a bent radius, or spoke. A wheel with bent spokes is normally buckled and no longer effective as a wheel.

Through that contact area you have to learn to swing the club along that broad white line 12 in (30.4 cm) in length and parallel to, or on, your target line. You will now appreciate how important your first golf swing routine, aiming, is.

Look at the photos of seventeen-year-old Barry Winton, one of my young protégés swinging through contact and along that white line. This line demands co-ordination of clubhead, hands and eyes which, if you do not already possess, you will acquire with practise. You should use that white line (mentally) with every shot you play. It is one of the few things you *must* take on the course. When you look at the photos of these professionals you cannot fail to observe their

All three stars in the photos on these pages, Gary Koch (top row) Greg Norman (left) and Lanny Wadkins (bottom row) have a number of common factors: (1) Note the flexed to left-right knee, the hip rotation and the right shoulder turning into the swing. (2) The head is centred so that the left cheek has been held to the right side of the golf ball, even after the ball has gone, because as yet the mind has not received the 'ball gone' message. (3) When the head does turn to target, this is where they expect the ball to go. (4) The swing is high at the finish. (5) The maypole brings the shaft at right angles to target line. (6) The right knee has ended the right side *return* by touching the left knee and the right heel is raised. All the weight is on the left foot at the end of the swing.

These young students of mine show exemplary forward extension and body *return*. In the top two photos a one-year golfer is gradually gaining speed control.

Above, an experienced student moves very accurately at high speed. Right and above right are of a single figure handicap-player who has a veritable superstar swing.

knees driving low through contact. They have been doing this since they heralded the change of swing direction. The left knee has been semicircling in a counter-clockwise direction while the right knee has bent into the left knee.

By swing finish, the right knee nearly, if not completely, touches the left leg and in most cases the left leg is finally extended as it takes all the body weight.

The right heel has come up from its inside to left starting point and the sole of the foot is at right angles to the ground, which helps the balance. At the final position the waist angle they started with has probably spiralled a little in response to the left leg straightening. But where the left knee has not completely straightened (this is not uncommon among the best players), the original waist angle could well have been retained. The plane will have been retained and the three o'clock plane check, like the nine o'clock check on the backswing, will ascertain this. The belt buckle is already facing target at this stage. High hands are a common finishing factor. In many cases the naked eye misses this because of the speed of the swing, but the camera captures it.

Top photo shows an enviable high finish. The student in the photo above is obviously a strong player but who would imagine that the one on the left is an absolute beginner?

All these players have a high standard of swing shape and pace, which suggests the superstar swing is not beyond the achievement of the house-wife, businessman, and craftsman.

The 'maypole' effect absorbs the remaining energy and is quite spontaneous. The speed of the swing will have increased with its progress and this is impossible to illustrate. The fastest part of the swing is from the clubhead's break through the golf ball's resistance to that high finish.

All very well for the superstars, but how can the ordinary Club golfer perform these athletic gyrations. Take a look at the photos of the ordinary golfers I have interspersed with the professionals. The ordinary golfer can make them. So can you.

Top row: All players have well-framed finishes. The player on the right has a high handicap with high skill; on the far right is a beginner. Pro Simon Hobday (below and below right) shows the almost cynical dash of a cavalier with his whiplash maypole, but he has obvious overall control in his forward extension, which stamps him as a highly successful tour pro. His speed of movement, which has nothing to do with hurry or effort, is most impressive.

Above: two of my many enthusiastic students who take their golf very seriously. They can be seen to be shaping up really well with high swing finishes. Their dedication to the mechanics is exemplary and from this they will soon acquire their feel for the movement. Remember, *you get the feel from the mechanics*. Not *the mechanics from the feel*.

Gordon Brand jnr. (middle row) and Kuramoto (below) have patently acquired the feel of the movement from the mechanics and now work from a basis of controlled awareness. They finish high, habitually.

Swing energy is finally dissipated in what I call a maypole finish or flourish. Some players who still have surplus energy at this stage will also recoil, but in my opinion there is the shadow of control loss when recoil takes over. A maypole looks cosmetically polished and contained.

Above left: This player has for years been a keen student of mine and still is. She shows a maypole in keeping with her accurately presented swing shape and swing speed. Above: Another of my students endowed with fanatical determination, has equal rights for the credit that Severiano Ballesteros has for a fine professional swing conclusion.

CONTACT ERRORS

As a human being you can commit seven different sins a day. As a golfer you are only liable to commit six different golfing sins. Before you run away with the idea that you will make only six mistakes every time you play golf, I must say that in the beginning stages you will repeat those mistakes more than you will enjoy making them. You will appeal to the people with whom you are playing, 'What am I doing wrong?'. As the mistakes recur, with agonizing regularity, you will plead for assistance with the same desperate frequency. You will be lavished with advice not only from your playing partners, but also from their caddies, and the players and their caddies ahead of you. What is more, if you have to wait long enough, also by the players and their caddies coming up behind! More than this, each adviser will offer a totally different cure for the same fault. It is as well that having forewarned you of the likelihood of this plethora of advice, I should forearm you, so that you will have no need of it! You will be able to cure yourself with the knowledge you derive from the way the ball flies. This is called feed-back.

There are six contact faults on the face of the golf club, and they produce six different types of golf-ball flights. *The only spot from which a perfect shot can be struck is in the centre of the club face.* Any shot that is struck away from the centre will tend not only to fly in the wrong direction, but also to lose distance. The six faults are as follows:

1. A ball contacted below centre will produce a low shot (a thin shot) or one that runs along the ground (a topped shot). The clubhead has been too high off the ground on contact and is corrected by the hands travelling lower to the ground through the contact area. The left side of the face should be held to the right side of the ball until the ball has gone.

2. A ball contacted above centre will produce a fat shot, or the ground has been

contacted before the ball. The ball will be lobbed or too high and of very short distance. Correct this by keeping your hands ahead of the clubhead through contact.

3. A ball contacted on the toe will tend to produce a curved-to-the-left flight (draw or hook) and is cured by holding the heel of the club to the ball at assembly and taking the forward swing path slightly more inside to out to correct the excessive 'inside-to-*you* path' of the return swing, which brings the toe to the ball.

4. A ball contacted on the heel of the club will produce a curved-to-the-right flight (a fade or a slice – the latter, a more intense curve than the former). The reverse cure for a toe shot applies here. Hold the toe of the club to the ball and track your hands nearer to you on the return swing than they were on the backswing. You will never shank (hit the ball with the neck of the club) if you strike the ball on the toe of the club.

5. A ball contacted with the face of the club 'open' or pointing to the right of target line, will either hit the ball straight to the right, or produce a fade or a slice. A straight shot to the right is called a 'pushed' shot. Clockwise rotation of the hands and arms has in this case been substituted for counter-clockwise rotation through the ball. A little more pressure of the last three left-hand fingers usually corrects this, but if this does not do the job, 'hood', the clubface, that is, hold the face of the club more down to the ground on the backswing.

6. A ball contacted with the face of the club turned in, 'closed', or to the left of target line will either pull (a straight shot to the left), or hook (a curving-to-the-left shot) it could even produce a mixture of the two, a pulled hook – straight first and swerving left at the end of the flight. The cure is to keep your hands leading the clubhead through contact.

These contact errors normally need

only a 'one off' correction, but try again if you are not successful the first time and, when you have corrected, you can assume the correction will stick without any further emphasis. No major swing change has been involved. The ball flight cannot lie. You are not guessing. The corrections should be made at your normal swing speed.

Let us nip over into that rough for a few minutes and try a spot of trouble shooting there!

Top left: A ball contacted on the toe.
Top right: A ball contacted on the heel.
Centre left: A ball contacted above centre.
Centre right: A ball contacted below centre.
Bottom left: A ball contacted on the closed face.
Bottom right: A ball contacted on the open face.
While slicing is the most common fault in the Club golfers' ranks, 'socketing' or hitting the ball in the neck of the club is the most distressing. Quite simply you must understand that this is merely temporary loss of control of the swing path of the forward swing. You are taking the path outside the normal one so that the heel or neck (further into the heel) of the club is brought into contact with the golf ball. Cure this by bringing the toe of the club into the ball. You will then be tracking more inside, enough to correct the amount of 'outside tracking' error. Practise missing the ball on the outside of it, then on the inside of it, and then tracking on the middle line where the ball is. You are gradually regaining that forward swing path control.

DIFFICULT SHOTS

Out of the Rough

The rough terrifies eighty percent of golfers. It is allowed to grow there for that reason. I am going to give you a formula for at least making it easier to get out of the rough. (There is of course the penal one of losing your ball and going back to where you played the lost one and then playing another with the addition of a penalty stroke.)

It may seem superfluous to warn you to carefully mark a spot or area near to where you saw the ball flying. Too often, because the shot you just played has not flown down the middle of the 'fairway', that smoothly cut area flowing attractively between rough grass and perhaps woodland, from tee to green, you will turn away in disgust and lose sight of the errant sphere's landing. A lot of golf balls are lost that way. A professional may feel just as disgusted with his hook or slice, but he will watch that ball like a hawk. He has no intention of throwing good money away.

The ball will tend to roll into a depression. You can count yourself lucky if you find a good lie in the rough, but don't be tempted to take liberties with a ball that seems to be sitting prettily on top of the undergrowth. I'll deal with this pitfall, as indeed it could be to the uninitiated, later.

Mostly you are going to have to negotiate with the ball lying snugly in the strong spiky grass like an egg in a bird's nest. It will look impossible to you at first and all the hacking and ploughing you will do would only tend to embed it further. Seventy percent of these rough shots need a deep-face sharp-bladed iron. Your wedge, if it has a narrow thin sole, or your 9-iron would be the club to select. Now, the longest shot you could play with either of these clubs would be in the region of 110 yd (100.5 m) and that would be from smooth fairway turf with minimum resistance. From .the long tough rough

grass with the ball at the base of the stalks you could calculate a maximum distance of 75 yd (68.5 m) and in many cases down to a maximum of 50 yd (45.7 m) or even less than that. If the green was 150 yd (137 m) away, you should discount reaching it. The middle of the fairway would be the next consideration, where you would have a better chance of reaching the green with the next shot. You should then take the nearest direction to the fairway. What is more, if the rough extends so far that it would be impossible to reach the fairway, except by playing back towards the tee, then you must play backwards and hope to reach the green with your next shot by using a longer club. In short, you cut your losses.

It is not possible to swing directly through the jungles of tiger grass that festoon a lot of golf courses unless you are some species of superman and superstar combined. You have to make contact with the ball by a route in which you are

minimally involved with the foliage. You do this by bringing the club more steeply onto the ball than you would for a normal shot. You can achieve this by:

1. Increasing the grip pressure to stop the clubhead from being twisted by any grass you may encounter.

2. Playing the shot with the ball in a line with a spot to the *right* of centre of your feet. It could even be opposite your right heel if you require an even more steep descent to avoid the grass entwining itself around the neck of your club and hopelessly deflecting it.

3. Making an exaggeratedly vertical backswing as opposed to your normal one horizontal – a little more wrist action and a little earlier too, will help to steepen your backswing.

4. Keeping more weight on your left foot than you would for a fairway or tee shot and by squatting more with your knees.

5. Pulling down with your hands leading the clubhead and continuing relentlessly.

Now, what about that 'rough' situation where the ball is sitting on top of a mass of folded-over grass, bent by wind and rain? Even if it looks tempting don't be lured into the trap of 'having a go' at it. You will more than likely plough through the undergrowth and the ball will fall into the hole of your own making.

For this shot take anything up to a 5-iron (if you need that distance, the longer clubs are more difficult to control), and assemble for a normal shot but hold the clubhead slightly higher than normal, above the top half of the ball. In other words, hold it as though you were going to make a deliberate top (hitting the top of the ball with the base of the clubhead), and then swing normally. You will find that the spontaneous extension of your arms as you swing through the ball will bring the centre of the clubface where it should be, into the back of the golf ball. It shouldn't be too difficult to find an area of rough in which to practise.

Intended Slice

Trees abound most inland courses and you are going to be a lucky golfer never to have to play from behind them. They can be literally insuperable hazards, impossible to get over. You may find a space through the branches but not the trunks. However, you can go around those trunks!

Suppose your ball is behind some trees that are in the way of a straight path to the green on the right, as you face the green. You can plan to fly the ball out to the fairway and make it curve to the right towards the green. It's quite simple. Aim your clubface to the green on your right (the clubface will be 'open') and your feet to the fairway on your left. Swing normally along your footline and for the first 50 yd (45.7 m) or so of its flight your ball will reach the fairway and when it loses its forward drive, the rightward spin will take over and it will fly to the green. No swing change will have been necessary for this deliberate slice.

Intended Hook

When the reverse applies and the trees obscure the green on your left, you hold the clubface to your target, leftward in this case (the clubface will be 'closed') and your feet will be lined up towards the fairway on the right. Swing normally along your footline and in its initial flight the ball will fly straight to the fairway. When the leftward spin takes over, the ball will change course and fly leftward to the green. You have played a deliberate hook without a swing change.

69

Uphill

You won't have far to walk on most golf courses before you encounter an uphill lie (when your ball is lying on an uphill slope) to the green. The chances are that you will fly the ball to the left if you play this one straight to the target. You should aim to the right and take a club more than you would for the same distance on level ground. Have the ball slightly left of centre at assembly. Neutralize the pull of gravity, which is down the slope, by holding your right foot and leg more in towards your left leg at the start of the swing and hold this support in to the left all the way to the top of your backswing, which should ideally be a trifle shorter than normal. The photos clearly demonstrate these points as the variable mat indicates the slopes.

Downhill

There is bound to be a downhill shot to play if there is an uphill one. The reverse of the uphill formula applies here. There is a tendency for the ball to fly to the right, so aim to the left. Counter the pull of gravity by utilizing the more into-the-right support of the left foot and leg. Have the ball nearer your right foot at assembly. Take a club one less than you would on level ground. Track your hands down the slope through contact as shown in the action photos.

Standing Below the Ball

There is a formula for striking a ball when it is above your feet, too. Without compensations, the ball would fly to the left with a curving flight. Therefore, your aim should be to the right. To stop yourself from falling backwards down the slope, lean a little towards your toes. Hold the club lower down the grip than you normally do and control the length of the backswing.

Winds

A strong wind against you can reduce your flight distance by as much as a third. You are going to need a long club for the distance between you and your target. To keep the ball flight lower, place your feet so that the ball is to the right of centre. This position is excellent, too for playing under low tree branches, but we use a straight-faced iron club. Cross-winds can obviously be allowed for by aiming right for a right-to-left wind and left for a left-to-right wind. There's another way, too especially with your driver: for a left-to-right wind aim straight but have your clubface turned into the left a little at assembly and swing normally. Swing normally, no matter what the direction or strength of the wind might be. Tend to lean against it so that it does not blow you off balance. Don't fight it, *use* it.

Perhaps the most formidable hazard you will encounter on every golf course you play, because you will take it with you is *concentration*. As it is impossible to give any subject or movement your undivided attention for more than a fraction of a second, it is therefore necessary to practise your movement sequence until it becomes habit. This reduces the amount of swing concentration and considerably shortens your concentration time.

Standing Above the Ball

When the ball is below your feet, expect it to fly to the right and compensate for this by aiming left and this time, to allow for gravitational pull, have more pressure than usual towards your heels. Stand a little nearer to the ball to slightly reduce the slope, and swing away.

The skilled player has made a habit of his swing and should be aware of his feel and judgement. His main concerns are which club to use and in which direction to aim. This will occupy no more than half a minute per shot. He then switches off and until the next shot he enjoys the scenery and perhaps pleasant thoughts of past successes. Use the following four pointers for concentration on your next game; I quote from Irv Schloss:

1. Reduce advanced apprehension and thoughts of the game you are going to play; keep your thoughts elevated and positive.

2. When you approach your ball to play your shot, make your assessment routine: Targets, bunkers and hazards, which will suggest direction and distance, to ascertain club selection. Go with your first choice, unquestionably. This is being positive.

3. Make your aim, grip, stance and posture routine with every shot. Bring your eyes from the target to the ball and clubface.

4. Use the imaginary 12 in (30.4 cm) white line I introduced earlier in the book and the co-ordination between your hands and eyes will certainly direct the clubhead along the line to your target, and then get back to enjoying your achievement in overcoming this obstacle.

SHORT GAME

When you drive off the tee, the centre of the fairway is not necessarily always the best target. You will obviously choose the spot that will make your second shot easier, and this might not mean the longest possible drive, either.

For similar reasons it is not always policy to aim directly for the flag on all your approach shots. It is advisable to play for the 'fat' of the greens; this would be mostly in the centre of the green for shots of over 100 yd (91.4 m). For shots of less than 100 yd, which come under the heading of approach shots, down to any shot off the green that could be termed 'pitch shots', providing there is a tolerable reception area to take the pitch and roll of the ball, it is quite economical to aim for the flag. Wind and weather promote differences from day to day and are obviously brought into account.

But let us wander back to the practice ground where we can really learn the simple art of the approach and pitch shots. Very few Club golfers really know how to vary the length of a shot, yet it is simple, like anything else, when you know how.

The not-so-experienced player will take a few months being able to make the distance differences between each iron club, but that time can be reduced by practising the short shot variations correctly and thus acquiring the constant rhythm that is the key to hitting a number 5-iron further than a number 7-iron, and a number 3-iron further than a number 5-iron and so on, up or down the scale.

It would be an over-simplification to say that if you swing at the same rhythm with every club you will get the different lengths the clubs are supposed to make. It is more accurate to say that if you *allow* the differences in the clubs to affect your swing rhythm then you will get the shot distance differences. For example, a number 7-iron which is approximately 36 in (914 mm) long and weighs about

fifteen and three-quarter ounces (446.5 g), will allow you X swing speed and because of its weight and face angle will fly the ball fairly high and a distance of approximately 140 yd (128 m) (average Club golfer); whilst a number 5-iron, which is approximately 37 ins (939.8 mm) long and weighs about fifteen and a quarter ounces (432.3 g) will allow you, because of its longer shaft and lighter weight than the 7-iron, a 2-X speed, and because of its less-angled clubface it will fly the ball lower than the 7-iron and approximately 20 yd (9 m) further, hypothetically 160 yd (146.3 m).

When it comes to those limited distances, however, from 100 yds (91.4 m) down, we must use the shortest

clubs, the wedge and the sand-iron. Having said that let me add that length variations can also be made with the 6, 7, 8 and 9-irons, even the 5-iron under some circumstances other than the optimum you would get from a full swing.

When you have virtually run out of clubs, you must resort to cutting down the length of your swing in order to shorten your shot. You do this by first of all deciding the length of the shot needed to reach that flag. Supposing it were 60 yd (54.8 m). It is possible that you would need a half swing with your wedge. Think of a large clock behind you, better still look at the 'clock' I have made on the pictures on page 76. A half swing would be from six o'clock (assembly) to nine

o'clock on the backswing and returning through six o'clock continuously to three o'clock on the forward swing. That would be swing completion.

My model, in this case Billy Knowles, has done just that in the pictures. It is likely that for the average golfer the ball will pitch about 60 yd (54.8 m) with a swing of this distance. You can only find out by measuring it. Have a formula for this too. Check how many normal steps you take for 10 yd (9.14 m). Measure the result of your nine to three shot by stepping out the distance your ball has gone.

It would be your number of steps for every 10 yd (9.14 m). You may find that the distance you have gone is more than 60 yd (54.8 m). So it would need a shorter swing distance for 60 yd and you would then try eight o'clock on the backswing to four o'clock on the forward swing. Note well that the forward swing is *always* as long as the backswing. It could also be less than 60 yd for your nine to three shot, which means, a longer swing distance, so you would try ten o'clock back, to two o'clock forwards. But measure carefully all the clock distances with your wedge, down to seven to five and up to eleven to one. Put them in your note book. Check the same swing lengths distances with your 6, 7, 8, 9 and sand-irons. Do not, by the way, make these measurements on the course. They should be made under normal, calm conditions, on your practice ground. You should check all your club distances there.

The swing technique is very much like a pendulum, with the forward swing equal in length to the backswing. Use a rather narrower stance than you would

Palmer's eight to four swing (left) is merely the contact area segment of the big swing. The bending of both knees to target helps the forward swing to correctly respond. Start to play the short shot before embarking on the long ones, although this will take you longer to get on the course. No matter how perfect your short shots are you can't really play every shot out there with a wedge, whereas you can 'scramble' your short shots if your long game is reasonable.

Faldo, (above) too, plays a miniature big swing for his nine to three shots. It is worth noting how he maintains his extension or the radius of the swing throughout the semicircle. It is a simple movement. Hand and arms back with no weight transference. Hands and arms through with all the weight transferred via the knees to the left foot. Head and waist angle help to hold the central hub.

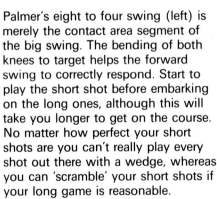

The clock speaks for itself! But I must remind you that you take your hands to the (imaginary) numbers and not the clubhead. The clubhead will extend beyond the numbers progressively, as you increase the 'times' or the swing length, for example, from seven up to eleven, and from five up to one.

for a full swing but with the same equivalent distribution of pressure between both feet and knees. Hold the club at the bottom of the grip for a seven to five swing and only a little higher for the eight to four swing whilst the nine to three

swing would be gripped in the middle of the club grip, the ten to two and the eleven to one would be gripped almost at the top of the grip.

For the seven to five swing (it is *hands* to seven by the way, the clubhead goes a little further) there would be little if any wrist response and no pressure or weight change from assembly to backswing completion. You then need to swing your hands and arms forward ahead of the clubhead through the ball, the clubhead may catch up with your hands at five o'clock, let your knees flex a little along the same forward-to-target path as your hands. Your head is held centrally just behind the ball position. The shoulders are passive.

The same applies to the eight to four length swing and the nine to three. You may well feel the wrists wanting to angle or bend. Do not inhibit this, but confine the pivotal points of the wrist break to the *base of the thumbs*. You will also experience some shoulder coil but it will be nothing like that of the *big* swing. No attempt to straighten this wrist angle is necessary on the forward swing. It all happens with the reaction of centrifugal force and the flow of the forward swing. The ten to two swing will involve you with a little more wrist angle, a little more trunk coil, and a little more leg or knee response on the return swing as will the eleven to one swing, which is nearly the *big* swing again.

What about that rhythm? It really comes under the physics law of circular motion. There is no need to manufacture acceleration, it is a natural, physical phenomenon. As there is a change in direction from the original direction (from backswing to downswing), any attempt to enhance this by flicking or applied effort in the 'contact area' will inhibit or reduce the effects of this acceleration and cause a slowing down of the swing. In other words you *allow* the speed or acceleration to take over. It is, or should be, quite spontaneous.

There is a special shot to play *over* those sandbunkers and water hazards. It is called a 'feathered shot'. Play it with a sand-iron. It is an eleven to one length swing played from beginning to end, in *slow motion*. The ball will fly almost as slowly as the swing and come to rest like a poached egg on heavily buttered toast. It does need practice.

Try a 'Paul Runyan' if you are of a nervous disposition on those shots around 10 yd (9.14 m) from the green, but over a sandbunker. Assemble as for a putt, but use a sand-iron. Bow both your elbows out, make a pendulum-like putting stroke with your wrists held firm and see your ball pop up and over the hazard to land safely onto the putting surface.

Alas, you are not going to avoid all those sand traps. We'll go with ex-tour player Tim Huyton and see how best to get out of them.

The 'Paul Runyan' is effectively demonstrated by Billy Knowles. Especially note there is no shift of weight or pressure on the backswing. There is no flexing or unflexing of the wrists on the backswing or forward swing respectively.

SAND SHOTS

I have seen the professionals using putters out of *sand* where there is no overhang and under some conditions, where the sand is wet or just firm, as opposed to the normal soft bunker sand, they will play as for the short pitch, assuming it is a greenside bunker, from turf, so the length of the swing will be ascertained by the length of the shot required.

For long bunker shots where the ball is sitting on top of the sand and if there is adequate space to clear the lip, they will play whatever club might be required for the distance. When necessary, they will even use a fairway wood played like a fairway shot.

If the ball is embedded in the face of the bunker or on a downhill slope in the foot of the bunker, the professionals like anyone else must play the *explosion* shot to be sure of playing the next one from a grassy lie.

The explosion shot is the accepted 'safest' bunker shot of any of the aforementioned or any that might be extemporized by players with enthusiastic initiative. This shot is mainly played with a sand-iron. If you look at the sand-iron in the picture on the opposite page you will see that it has a flange or a broad base. The 'leading edge' or the bottom of the clubface is quite sharp to make the initial cut into the sand, while the broad base slides through the sand under the ball.

When the ball is partially buried in wet or firm sand, it is better to use a club with a not-so-broad base, which will more easily cut through the tougher sand than the deeper flanged sand-iron, such as a wedge or a 9-iron. There is no difference in swing method.

The 'foot shuffle' you see the pros make as they take their stance, has two uses, one is to make sure their feet are firmly embedded, and the second to test the consistency of the sand.

They aim left of the target with

everything from feet to shoulders but the clubface is held on to target, or slightly 'open', pointing a little to the right of it. As you are going to strike the sand before the ball, have the ball positioned that much to left of the centre of your feet. Never ground the club in the sand before you start the swing. Swing back unhurriedly with an earlier wrist cock than for a normal shot, but with double the length of swing you would make for a similar distance from grass. Without altering the face of the club, make your swing path follow the leftward orientation of your body. If the clubhead overtakes your hands, it must not be until well after the swing has gone through contact.

Practice by making 'golf ball pies' in your practice bunker. In the sand around each ball, draw a 2-in (5-cm) circle. This is the golf ball pie. Practice taking *the whole pie* out of the bunker with each shot.

Counteract a buried or half-buried ball and one that is deep into the overhang by holding the clubface leftward or turned in. Again, a wedge or 9-iron will cut more incisively into the sand than a sand-iron. The body aim and swing path is as before, and the hands lead the clubhead even more, to plunge the clubface deeply into the sand before the ball – and up pops the ball. We are on the green!

You have played the shot in golf which requires the slowest swing. The slowest swing but as continuous as the fastest swing.

Opposite: Tim Huyton aims himself left as he holds the sand iron face to target. This sounds very easy but you will automatically compensate for the apparent anomaly. With *practice* you will be able to swing back normally like Tim without compensation taking place (left).

The wrist cock will be somewhat earlier than a normal shot, to deepen the arc of the swing so that you can take that golf ball pie (below) with a descending approach. If you think about it, another unique point about the sand shot is having to take the ground before the ball.

As you become more disciplined to one part of you facing one way, and holding the club face in the opposite direction, your sojourns in the sand will become more brief and your follow-through more like Tim Huyton's (below left).

PUTTING

The superstars will place more importance on the distance of a putt than the direction. 'If you can't see a line on a green, you shouldn't be there', they say. Well, they mean playing the tour.

The better you play the long putts, the easier the short ones are going to be. There is little point in looking for any but the very obvious side slopes on these. It is only the last quarter or less, of the long putt that will take a side slope if there is one. If you can't see a slope, play the putt as a straight one. If there is a visible side slope, assess the point where the ball would lose impetus, and play a straight putt to that point.

Uphill putts obviously need to be struck more firmly than downhill putts, but you should aim to be no more than 6 in (15.2 cm) past the hole on an uphill putt and no more than 2 ft 6 in (762 mm) past the hole on a downhill putt.

Be more concerned with putting against the grain and with the grain than across the grain when assessing strength. The grain is the direction in which the grass grows. On very fast downhill slopes you will hit the ball more softly by striking it on the toe of your putter.

A ball will normally run down a side slope but there are some locations where mountains and rivers influence putts regardless of the natural slopes. The ball seems to be magnetized by these. The locals will be delighted to tell you about their special phenomenon.

I have picked Tom Purtzer, winner of the 1984 Phoenix Open, to portray the common putting factors of the superstars (you can compare him with Craig Stadler and Lee Trevino). He uses the reverse overlapping grip in which the forefinger of the left hand overlaps the little finger of the right hand. *Both* thumbs are placed on top of and directly along the centre of the grip. There are no knuckles of the back of the left hand showing.

Tom's upper arms are grooved to his

sides and his elbows are bent to make a cradle of his forearms and hands. His left wrist will start and remain quite firm throughout the putt as he moves the cradle back and forth. He is assembled with a narrower than normal swing stance, but he is well balanced. As in the big swing, both knees are in a little to the ball and in a little to each other. The pressure is fifty-fifty between both feet and there will be no change of this and no weight shift as he moves the cradle. The putter head is held low to the ground and taken slightly inside the target line on the backswing. He returns it straight through to target and elevates it progressively after contact. He, like you, will enjoy watching

the ball disappear into the cup. Sinking a good length putt soothes the pain of a missed tee or fairway shot.

Both Craig Stadler and Lee Trevino reveal exactly the same common factors of the simple putting technique. They, with Tom Purtzer and all the other superstars, owe a great deal of their success to the brilliance of their putting skill.

You may not be able to practise every day, but you may find time during the odd winter evening to putt into a drinking glass on the lounge carpet. If you repeat the superstar putting movement often enough it will become a habit.

Stadler (opposite), Purtzer (below) and Trevino (bottom) have another important common factor: Their eyes are directly above the golf ball throughout the stroke. As the slopes on the greens curve the ball, they make every putt a straight one.

Trevino once said that the backswing of a putt is the only swing where an inside path should be taken – a statement that provides more food for thought.

EXERCISES

I am frequently asked, 'What are the best exercises for golf?'. Too often, I suspect, the questioner is looking for an easy substitute for the hard work involved in straightforward practice.

To give the benefit of the doubt, if there has been little or no reward as yet from practising, I must confess that I do believe sensible and moderate exercises can enhance practice and some reward could be forthcoming.

For some particular weaknesses specific forms of exercises could turn those weaknesses into strengths. I am reminded of a former assistant of mine who had not very active legs. Consequently, his golf swing was dominated too much by his shoulders. Being young and particularly fit he could take quite strenuous exercises without danger of muscular or organic injury. I got him to run up and down a very steep, 50-yd (45.7 m) slope, starting at three times a day and progressing to twelve times a day while carrying a golf bag containing two sets of clubs across his shoulders and held there with both hands.

On the first and subsequent few days, I have never seen a human being so exhausted, but he grimly stuck at it. I got

him to play a daily round of golf starting at 7.30 am, running between shots. He was joined by another of my assistants, Glyn Rowland and a former young Swedish professional Mats Wahlstrom. They completed the rounds by 9 am and each marked a card, at first they scored in the low nineties but after a few days they were scoring in the seventies.

The assistant in question became quite a good golfer and competitor, winning a number of local titles.

In his case, the exercises strengthened the weak area and while the main source of his skill did come from practising hard regularly, these exercises must also have contributed.

As a generalization, I certainly would not prescribe such violence. In fact, I believe that gentle callisthenics – which are exercises for cultivating gracefulness and strength combined – are, with regularly spaced practice that avoids fatigue and boredom, the ideal combination for improving your golf skill. Golf swinging is an exercise which, if carried out in the right sequence, must obviously improve your performance.

Take a longish bathroom towel, tie a

knot in the end of it and swing this twenty to thirty times a day – only in your garden or empty garage, don't try it in your bathroom! I know of nothing else better for making you swing like the pro stars. Look at the swing sequence demonstrating the towel exercise. You can see for yourself the effects of inertia, centripetal and centrifugal forces responding to the movement you are compelled to make to stop the towel entwining itself about you. You will actually get the true feel of the superstar forward drive movement, which they do so skilfully with real clubs. What is more, having experienced the 'feel' with the towel, it will not be too difficult for you to transfer it to a golf club.

The pivotal exercise in my opinion is the most important pre-practice and pre-play exercise of all. Wedge a club between your elbows and in the small of the back. Take a golfing stance and turn on the backswing until the head of the club points to the ball, re-turn until the butt of the club points to the ball. This is a wonderful muscle memory jogger for the trunk pivot. The photos clearly demonstrate this exercise, used widely by the golfing elite.

Bottom row: The Towel Swing.

The knotted towel presents the most exciting golf swing exercise yet devised. You simply have to swing correctly to make the towel behave correctly. You are compelled to allow the natural responses to take over.

On the backswing the physics law of inertia and continuity compel wrist and right elbow flexion. Good centring, too, is an automatic reaction. You will rotate as if you are encased in a tube that is tilted to contain your trunk angle.

Your hands must be leading the towel to achieve the Hogan-like position in picture number **4**. This really is a perfect demonstration of centripetal and centrifugal force. The whole of the swing is subjected to the physics law of circular motion. When the directional change is effected the then forward movement

is continued unimpeded. There should be no attempt to take from it or to add to it. The knotted towel demands just this. Transmit this feel to a golf club and you have the superstar movement. In my opinion, the towel sequence is one of the most revealing of any golf-swing sequence I have ever photographed.

Trunk Rotation Reminder

My model here is Audrey Cooke. Both Jack Nicklaus and Calvin Peete are addicts of the prior-to-practice trunk rotation exercise. They are not alone. Many of the tour players participate in this muscle memory jogger. With all the good intent in the world it is so easy to forget to turn or to take the easy way out and just hope to turn, and die in despair.

The backswing coil in particular always takes up a lot of energy,

which most players will naturally, albeit unintentionally, avoid. 'Oh I thought I turned', but the wish is further than the fact. Nine times out of ten, the lift on the forward swing is only the weak-kneed response to the lift or lack of turn on the backswing. You have got to feel it. If you don't feel it, you are not doing it.

Remember, wedge the club along the small of your back between your elbows, butt end of shaft to the right, head end to left. Maintaining your normal assembly waist angle throughout the swing, turn or coil until the head of the club points to the ball. Never mind those muscles you were never aware of before, they won't crack. Now you return until the butt end of the grip points to the ball. That's the way you should always turn. Note how those legs react. The right knee nudges the left, at the end.

Swinging two clubs as one, will vividly convey swing extension, and the *flow* of the forward swing. This also helps to build up your swing pace in the same way that running training in heavy boots speeds up running in light running shoes. Twelve swings daily, ideally, with the combination of wedge and sand-iron, but any two irons will do, are ample. It is excellent for a swing 'warm up' just before a game, when you cannot hit some practice shots because of lack of time or space. Photos below and below right.

On the practice ground I am a great believer in playing shots with one arm only. At first this will be rather traumatic. Stick at it, and soon you will be amazed at your own one-arm skill. Gunnar Mueller, one of Sweden's top ranking professionals, is a one-arm practice addict. He is seen in the photos opposite. It certainly strengthens your two-armed prowess.

Just hitting golf shots is excellent for strengthening your golf muscles and much more beneficial than a before-breakfast two-mile jog. When you are playing golf you are also getting the benefit of the best and most natural exercise there is, walking. You'll be walking pretty smartly too, to hold your position among the slickly moving golfers of today.

The advent of the buggy will of course reduce the amount of walking as it already has done in America but they take the view that this conserves your energy for playing the shots. Certainly, it opens golf courses for the not-so-fit.

The Two Club Swing
Below: Glyn Rowland my assistant and clubmaker demonstrates two club-swinging exercises for before a game or practising. Back and through swings are clearly shown coupled with the extension of the arms that the extra weight induces. The stronger readers may be tempted to use three or even more clubs, but keep it safely within your capacity. When you swing with one club after this, it's as light as a wand and produces similar golf shot magic. Note the left-arm extension on the backswing and both arms being stretched forward. It's a lazy way to practise. Twelve two-club swings have the same limbering-up effect of forty golf shots.

Six-second exercise
Reluctantly, I must confess to a certain amount of leaning to isometrics, though I have here reduced it to the absolute minimum because I feel there is a certain amount of physical risk involved and I do not want to jeopardize in any way the medical well-being of any of my readers. I do feel, however, that the amount of pressure needed to squeeze your club against the wheel of your trolley for *no more* than six seconds while you are awaiting your turn to tee off, will do you no harm and will even act as a reminder of the predominance of your hands over that of the clubhead; and if the theory of isometrics is correct, you will strengthen your forearms and hands considerably for the few six-second sessions you will surely find time for during each of your rounds of golf.

One-arm practice

One-armed practice is quite a marathon. The left-arm practice shows how important this swing radius member is. Note in middle right photo and below of left-arm contact how perfectly extended and firm the left arm and wrist are, underlining beyond a shadow of doubt, the key arm in the golf swing. Right-arm practice, top and middle left, however, still has its place and top right demonstrates the retention of the wrist angle. Even with the right arm only *there is no early hit or release*. The movement conforms completely to the law of circular motion and continues uninterruptedly from directional change to swing finish.

THREE
SUPERSTARS

Arnold Palmer

I first saw Arnold Palmer at St Andrews in 1960 at the Centenary Open, which was won by Kel Nagle with a score of 278. Palmer was second, one stroke behind. He won it the following year at Royal Birkdale and the year after that, in 1962, at Troon.

The first drive I ever saw him playing was from the seventeenth tee at St Andrews during a practice round for that Centenary Open.

After finishing my round, lecturer Doug Graham, who used to caddie for me in the Opens, and I, darted back from the seventeenth tee in time to see him play from there. He teed up, wasted no time, and with a coil that had to be seen to be believed, unleashed a fury I had never before observed in a human being. It was a cloudless deep blue sky. I watched the large American-size ball take off, screaming, low to high, on and on, until it was no longer visible, even to my sharp vision! He had literally driven the ball out of sight. We dashed along the rough before his playing companions had time to move and eventually spotted Palmer's ball tucked into the right side of the fairway, Doug Graham stepped out the distance it was from the green. In all, thirty-five paces. The length of the seventeenth at that time was 466 yd (426 m)! It was the only time I had ever seen, and I believe ever shall see, a ball fly out of sight.

Palmer's wide and firm stance gives him a secure base from which to turn and swing. It makes a strong link with the ground, which encourages the flow of centripetal force, which counter-balances the effects of centrifugal force. He has a waist angle. In other words, he is not standing bolt upright. Cheat a little here and follow the progress of that waist angle throughout his swing. It does not change until it spirals upwards. The very slight lowering of his head on the downward

part of the forward swing is due to both his knees driving low to target.

His left arm and shaft are not perfectly aligned, but this was a Hogan characteristic so that he could make a 'physical gain' through contact. The left wrist is slightly concave at assembly but by the time it reaches impact the left wrist is perfectly extended, in fact, slightly convex. It has gained on its start position, and in doing so has created energy. Palmer's backswing is a good example of what I describe as extension. He takes the whole triangle of both arms and 'responsive shoulders' back as it started, without contraction.

He gets wrist angle collection and right elbow bending towards the ground as a response to swing continuity and inertia.

The measure of his control comes from the late and slight raising of his left heel, his right leg held into centre and the back of his left hand in plane with his left wrist.

Leg response to the swing directional change and the brilliance of his wrist angle retention should be copied by all enthusiasts. Speed or flow should be allowed to progress without interruption. In Palmer's case, it does so to a reverse maypole rather than the conventional one.

Palmer now follows a very lucrative Senior Star's trail in the USA, with the stars of yesterday still in glittering constellation and drawing as much attention as the 'Big Tour' does.

Bernhard Langer

Bernhard Langer's assembly bears the Palmer, Jacklin, and Watson hallmark. The left hand and wrist are slightly concave. Switch to contact and there it is, that 'physical gain' that signals retention of radius and solid swing continuity.

Have no doubts in your mind, these are very rarely seen positions in Club golfers. Nevertheless, they should directly or indirectly be worked at, until the collapse has been repaired.

Langer, like Watson, Palmer and Jacklin, stands just as wide with his pressures correctly bedded. He has a good footing, a good hold on the ground – a base from which he can stretch and coil, to collect potential energy no less potent than theirs.

I make no apology for constantly repeating the common factor ingredients of the assembly. They are sixty percent of the golf swing and if these ingredients are only there in part, or are not present, there can be positively no hope of finding the missing ones in the optimum two seconds that the dynamic part takes.

Langer's knees drive pretty low through the forward swing and like his colleagues, who hit the ball so far, his hands travel near to his knees through contact.

From my first sight of him, Langer's speed has always impressed me. It is not as ferocious as Palmer's, nor yet quite as graceful or smooth as Jacklin's but it completes the cross-section. I observed him for a few years before his breakthrough, building up his reliable repetitive method. He works with a typical teutonic thoroughness and seriousness which has earned him his high-ranking position as one of Europe's leading professional players.

He didn't just appear at the top. Like many stars who have come and gone before him, his road was paved with dedication, willpower and hard work. I originally thought he had a low swing finish, but an early movie sequence I took of him revealed otherwise. It was all there! A high superstar follow-through from a well-sustained extension complementing the extraordinary distance he flies a golf ball.

Bernard Langer's left wrist position at impact is unbroken. Like his body, his arms, wrists, hands and club are rotating counter-clockwise as a unit, and as long as this happens he can safely lead the clubhead with his hands. You can be sure his clubhead will invariably track along that imaginary 12 in (30.4 cm) white line.

Tony Jacklin

It would not be completely true to say that Tony Jacklin swings exactly like Arnold Palmer. No two players swing exactly alike. Everybody is characterized by a distinguishing style. It is easy to pick out players on a golf course from a distance by their style. Their methods, as we have seen, require much deeper analysis.

And yet, look at Jacklin's assembly, his common factors, even to the slight leftward tilt to the ball with his head, are virtually identical to Palmer.

Look at the concave left wrist at the start; now, go forward to contact and we have a similar change in position. At contact his wrist has extended. He has made the same physical gain. Compare their grips. They are practically identical.

The stance widths can both be described as wide and the knee pressures are similar.

Jacklin takes the arms/shoulder triangle back in the same unbroken extension as Palmer. It must be logical to start the same and continue the same. They are both responding to the same machinery and must provoke the same responses.

There is no change of Tony's initial waist angle on the backswing, nor on the directional change. The trunk continues to uncoil unimpeded to swing finish. Jacklin's tendency to extend his right leg through contact would not be visible to the naked eye and to save you the futility of thinking you have spotted the Jacklin 'fault', let me say at once that this in no way affects his contact.

Compare his trunk coil with Palmer, the aligned left wrist and back of the left hand, and you are looking at the same progression of power. The same collection of potential energy. Jacklin's, like Palmer's transference of potential to kinetic energy, is of no mean proportion. He flies that golf ball a long way.

I have always said that Palmer has the most active left arm in the business. Jacklin comes a close second, as his unbroken swing wheel radius rips unhindered through contact.

In both men the right arm gives unstinted support to the left. That's what it is used for.

I have a film of Tony Jacklin taken when he won the British Open in 1969. The one shot that most impressed me was his second shot to the last green on the last round of the tournament. He probably played a 9-iron. On my clock system, it was a perfect ten to two swing. His judgement was perfect, even under the unique pressure of playing a second shot to a tightly bunkered green surrounded by thousands of spectators both in the

grandstand and surging in to close a ring around him.

The ball pitched and rolled to rest at 'pin high' a few yards from the hole. Two putts for the Open. His first putt finished 'dead' and I can still recall his jubilation as he tapped it in.

It is my sincere hope that you will be putting out many times on your own eighteenth green, having two putts, if not for the Open Championship, at least for the Monthly Medal. Perhaps one day it will be for the Club Championship and later on for an even more exaulted County Championship?

Tony Jacklin's backswing is characteristic of a sideways arms extension. Directional change is begun by his knees. This is a safer way of uncoiling the hips as opposed to a direct one.

NEWNES ALL COLOUR GUIDE

Golf